Beating Dyspraxia with a **Hop, Skip** and a **Jump**

of related interest

Can't Play Won't Play
Simply Sizzling Ideas to Get the Ball Rolling for Children with Dyspraxia
Sharon Drew and Elizabeth Atter
ISBN 978 1 84310 601 2

Understanding Dyspraxia
A Guide for Parents and Teachers
2nd edition
Maureen Boon
ISBN 978 1 84905 069 2
JKP Essentials Series

Understanding Motor Skills in Children with Dyspraxia, ADHD, Autism, and Other Learning Disabilities
A Guide to Improving Coordination
Lisa A. Kurtz
ISBN 978 1 84310 865 8
JKP Essentials Series

How to Help a Clumsy Child
Strategies for Young Children with Developmental Motor Concerns
Lisa A. Kurtz
ISBN 978 1 84310 754 5

Beating

Dyspraxia

with a **Hop**, **Skip** and a **Jump**

**A Simple Exercise Program
for Home and School**

Geoff Platt

Jessica Kingsley *Publishers*
London and Philadelphia

Extracts from Kirby and Drew 2003 on p.18–19, 24 and 26–27 are reproduced by permission of David Fulton
DSM material on p.21–22 is reproduced by permission of American Psychiatric Publishing, Inc.
Table 3.2 from N.A. Ratamess 2008 on p.66 is reproduced by permission of Human Kinetics
Extract from Schmidt and Wrisberg 2008 on p.69 is reproduced by permission of Human Kinetics
Extract from Macintyre on p.71 is reproduced by permission of David Fulton
Figure 4.13 from Widmaier *et al* 1990 on p. 84 is reproduced by permission of McGraw Hill
Figure 4.14 from Tucker 2000 on p.85 is reproduced by permission of EMS Publishing
Extracts from R. Martens 1981 on p.121-123 are reproduced by permission of Human Kinetics
Figures 4.2 and 4.5 drawn by Jenni Platt

First published in 2011
by Jessica Kingsley Publishers
116 Pentonville Road
London N1 9JB, UK
and
400 Market Street, Suite 400
Philadelphia, PA 19106, USA

www.jkp.com

Library of Congress Cataloging in Publication Data
Platt, Geoff, 1955-
Beating dyspraxia with a hop, skip, and a jump : a simple exercise program for home and school / Geoff Platt.
p. ; cm.
Includes bibliographical references.
ISBN 978-1-84905-171-2
1. Apraxia--Exercise therapy. 2. Motor ability in children. 3. Movement disorders in children. I. Title.
[DNLM: 1. Apraxias--therapy. 2. Child. 3. Exercise Therapy--
methods. 4. Motor Skills Disorders--therapy. WL 340]
RJ496.A63P53 2011
618.92'8552--dc22
2010042008

British Library Cataloguing in Publication Data
A CIP catalogue record for this book is available from the British Library

ISBN 978 1 84905 171 2

Printed and bound in Great Britain

Acknowledgements

I would like to start by thanking the man who has done the most to make this work happen, Dr John Sproule.

The research would not have been possible without the support of a number of schools in Croydon and I would like to express my appreciation for their support and assistance.

Gresham Primary School

Keston Primary School

Oval Primary School

Rowdown Primary School

Wolsey Primary School

I would also like to thank Dr Nikos Papadakis, who collaborated on the entropy research, Professor Mohsen Shafizadeh, who collaborated with the movement skills research and Mrs Signa Ashdown who came to my assistance on several cold winter days when there were just too many children for me alone!

Finally, to my family, for their love and support and their understanding for those times during my research when I was not around. To my wife, Annette and my daughters, Jennifer, Laura and Eleanor.

Contents

Preface

A number of observers have identified that children with dyspraxia have weak muscles, particularly in their fingers, hands and wrists. Despite these observations, and the fact that strength has been identified as improving the symptoms of those with cerebral palsy, whilst dyspraxia has been referred to as *minimal cerebral palsy*, only four pieces of research into the effects of strength and strength training on dyspraxia appear to have been published.

Between 1989 and 2001, an Australian sports physiologist by the name of Annette Raynor researched strength as an issue for children with dyspraxia and published two papers on the results of her research. She showed that there was a correlation between children with dyspraxia and children with poor isometric leg strength and showed that this was linked to poor muscle activation and co-activation.

In 1997 two superintendent physiotherapists in London, Michelle Lee and Graham Smith, decided to review a number of interventions that were being used across London hospitals to assist children with dyspraxia (Lee and Smith 1998). Parents, identifying that their children were experiencing movement difficulties, were taking their children to see the family doctor who was referring the children to the local hospital. At the hospital the doctors, lacking any firm guidance, were referring the children to physiotherapists or occupational therapists for support. The occupational therapists identified tasks that were troubling the children and then set about practising them. The physiotherapists had attempted a wide range of interventions and this review was an attempt to identify what worked and what did not.

Lee and Smith found that the best results were achieved when each child's movement skills were individually assessed and a professional judgement made about the likely causes so that an individualized strength training program could be designed. This program was performed five times each week under parental guidance, and once under the guidance of the physiotherapist in order to provide support for the parent and child.

In this way, Smith and Lee identified that they were able to achieve a 72 per cent reduction in the symptoms of dyspraxia experienced by the children after only eight weeks. Unfortunately, the cost of the intensive employment of specialist paediatric physiotherapists over a period of almost six months was found to be prohibitive and this intervention appears to have almost completely lapsed.

These excellent results seem to have been overlooked in recent years, as doctors, psychologists, neurologists and others have explored the workings of the human brain to find the causes of dyspraxia and a suitable intervention. Strength training has always been seen as an activity for grown men, rather than for children with movement difficulties. Few scientists knew much about strength training and no further research was conducted.

I am an experienced weightlifting coach and a teacher in primary and secondary schools as well as colleges and university. Recognizing the strength of previous research, I decided to seek a way to replicate the results of Lee and Smith using only the resources available at the local primary school: PE teachers, sports coaches, the school field or school hall, a gymnasium bench or a tree log and a tennis or squash ball. The result is a very simple exercise program, based on running, jumping and hopping, which can be safely undertaken by any child under the supervision of a teacher, sports coach or parent. It eliminates weakness, improves neural control of movement by improving muscle activation and ultimately reduces the symptoms of dyspraxia.

This book provides parents, sports coaches and teachers with a method to help children with dyspraxia to improve their movement skills. It will also encourage further research into an area that has provided positive results and to ensure that strength and muscle training are not overlooked for another ten years.

Part I

The Background

Chapter 1

What Is Dyspraxia?

Experts agree that over the period of the last century there has been a loss of movement skills among some children, so that a group now exists who may be described as clumsy and in need of support. They may knock into furniture, have difficulty writing and drawing and quickly gain a reputation for misbehaving.

These difficulties are usually first identified at school where children are seen by teachers and compared with others of a similar age and background and judgements can more easily be made than at home, where the children are seen in isolation within their family.

Of course, schools, like every other part of our society, are changing. Pressure from the government to raise standards in literacy, numeracy and science have compelled head teachers to increase the amount of time that children spend in the classroom and thereby reduce the time that they spend outside studying nature, exploring our environment and simply moving around freely.

Classrooms now contain a wide range of valuable, electronic equipment ranging from computers, televisions and videos to electronic whiteboards; some schools even provide each individual child with his or her own laptop computer on which to do schoolwork. With all this valuable equipment in the classroom it is clear to see that there is no room for clumsy children running around and knocking over the furniture, and that strict discipline needs to be enforced.

Teachers are caring people who work in teams in schools and when they began noticing that there was a problem with the movement skills of their children they started to talk about it with their colleagues and then, when they found no easy solution to the problem, to start writing papers that were published to wider groups of fellow teachers and other professionals. The professionals included in these discussions about children with movement difficulties include:

- teachers
- physical education specialists
- special educational needs coordinators (SENCO)
- educational psychologists
- social workers
- doctors/paediatricians
- orthopaedic surgeons
- speech and language therapists
- occupational therapists
- physiotherapists.

As the debate widened there was a need to give the condition a name and some of the names that teachers and other professionals gave the condition included, according to Boon 2010:

dyspraxia

clumsy child syndrome

developmental agnosia and apraxia

developmental coordination disorder (D.C.D.)

learning difficulties/disabilities/disorders

minimal cerebral palsy

minimal cerebral dysfunction

minimal brain dysfunction

minimal motor dysfunction

motor learning difficulties

neurodevelopmental dysfunction

perceptual/perceptuo-motor dysfunction

physical awkwardness

specific learning difficulties

sensori-motor dysfunction.

(Boon 2010, p.9)

The labels that were selected are interesting in that they reflect the way in which the condition was viewed. In the UK the term that has stuck is 'dyspraxia'. *Praxis* is the function by which we plan movement. If you want to catch a ball that is coming towards you, you need first to judge its distance from you, its trajectory and its speed. You then need to work out a way to get yourself underneath it as it comes to earth, by running towards it and placing your hands together under the ball and clamping them together at the exact second that the ball arrives between them.

If you were asked to explain these calculations on paper, few of us could do so, but most of us are able to do these calculations in our head and catch the ball at the same time! The name dyspraxia reflects a belief that the movement difficulties reflect an inability in those with the condition to perform this planning and therefore, to execute these movements.

In the United States, the condition is sometimes called 'developmental coordination disorder' (or DCD) to reflect that the condition is seen as a problem of growing children failing to make progress at the same rate as their peers. The word 'co-ordination' leaves the cause of the problem open to wider discussion than the UK equivalent of 'praxis'. However, 'dyspraxia' and 'developmental coordination disorder' are generally understood to be interchangeable terms and will be taken to refer to the same condition in this book.

Labelling a condition has the advantage that it acknowledges that a problem exists and assists in making applications for funding for research into a named condition rather than a more abstract problem. Unfortunately, it may also be seen as an excuse for poor behaviour by some families and as a justification for failing to attempt to raise standards. According to Kirby and Drew a label can mean:

> Acknowledgement for the parent of worries and concerns, and confirmation of the condition: allows others to see the parent as not just 'another over-anxious parent'.

> The provision of funds or services for the child.

> The provision of a cohort of individuals with signs and symptoms that may be useful for research.

> Allowing individuals working with the child to read up around the condition and consider what type of support is required.

> It may be used in legal cases as a reference point to consider one child's support compared to others.

> It may be used to plan service delivery or for baseline assessment and in-school remediation programmes.

> It may suggest negative connotations and may mean that individuals who come into contact with the child have preconceived ideas about the strengths and difficulties based on their experience of others with the same label they have come into contact with, who could even have been atypical.

> Placing children in very small boxes and not seeing them from all perspectives – this may lead to missing a diagnosis.

> The child perhaps ends up with many labels but not the right type of help.

> The child then being 'tattooed' for life with what they can't do rather than what they can do.

One label does not carry as much weight as another; for instance, medical labels may seem more important than educational ones (e.g. epilepsy versus dyslexia).

(Kirby and Drew 2003, pp.1–2)

At the same time as the researchers were labelling the condition they set out to list the symptoms of the disorder that they were witnessing. The most complete list of symptoms are grouped into lists below

The areas affected are:

- gross motor skills (these involve skills such as running, jumping and throwing)
- fine motor skills (these include tasks undertaken whilst sitting at a desk such as writing, drawing, putting pegs in a board)
- speech and language
- social skills
- attention and concentration
- learning
- visual motor skills.

The primary problems include:

- low muscle tone
- weak hands and fingers
- fast fatigue of the muscles
- poor joint stability
- inability to conceptualize movement, particularly across their midline
- inability to execute movements, particularly across their midline
- poor coordination
- poor balance

- poor attention
- inability to screen out the non-relevant
- poor proprioceptive feedback (poor awareness of own movement)
- poor tactile feedback (poor sensitivity to touch)
- overall lack of inhibition in the central nervous system (over-excitement of the central nervous system)
- hyperactivity
- poor eye movements.

The secondary problems of dyspraxia are:

- lack of confidence
- poor self-esteem
- refusal to participate
- avoidance
- frustration
- unhappiness
- loneliness
- becoming withdrawn
- acting the clown.

When the researchers had agreed that there was a problem that needed to be addressed, labelled it and drawn up a list of symptoms, they set about writing a definition for the disorder. A number of other professionals from a range of other specialisms have also attempted to define the condition. Although a number of definitions have been written, the one that is most authoritative and widely accepted is the one published by the American Psychological Association (APA) in the most recent version of their Diagnostic and Statistical Manual of Mental Disorder (DSM-IV) which appears opposite.

American Psychiatric Association

DSM-IV Description of DCD
Motor Skills Disorder
315.4 Developmental Coordination Disorder
Diagnostic features

The essential feature of Developmental Coordination Disorder is a marked impairment in the development of motor coordination (Criterion A). The diagnosis is made only if this impairment significantly interferes with academic achievement or activities of daily living (Criterion B). The diagnosis is made if the coordination difficulties are not due to a general medical condition (e.g., cerebral palsy, hemiplegia, or muscular dystrophy) and the criteria are not met for Pervasive Developmental Disorder (Criterion C). If Mental Retardation is present, the motor difficulties are in excess of those usually associated with it (Criterion D). The manifestations of this disorder vary with age and development. For example, younger children may display clumsiness and delays in achieving developmental motor milestones (e.g., walking, crawling, sitting, tying shoelaces, buttoning shirts, zipping pants). Older children may display difficulties with the motor aspects of assembling puzzles, building models, playing ball, and printing or handwriting.

Associated features and disorders
Problems commonly associated with Developmental Coordination Disorder include delays in other non-motor milestones. Associated disorders may include Phonological Disorder, Expressive Language Disorder, and Mixed Receptive-Expressive Language Disorder.

Prevalence
Prevalence of Developmental Coordination Disorder has been estimated to be as high as 6% for children in the age range of 5–11 years.

Course
Recognition of Developmental Coordination Disorder usually occurs when the child first attempts such tasks as running, holding a knife

and fork, buttoning clothes, or playing ball games. The course is variable. In some cases, lack of coordination continues through adolescence and adulthood.

Differential diagnosis

Developmental Coordination Disorder must be distinguished from motor impairments that are due to a general medical condition. Problems in coordination may be associated with specific neurological disorders (e.g., cerebral palsy, progressive lesions of the cerebellum), but in these cases there is definite neural damage and abnormal findings on neurological examination. If Mental Retardation is present, Developmental Coordination Disorder can be diagnosed only if the motor difficulties are in excess of those usually associated with the Mental Retardation. A diagnosis of Developmental Coordination Disorder is not given if the criteria are met for a Pervasive Developmental Disorder. Individuals with Attention-Deficit/Hyperactivity Disorder may fall, bump into things, or knock things over, but this is usually due to distractibility and impulsiveness, rather than to a motor impairment. If criteria for both disorders are met, both diagnoses can be given.

Diagnostic criteria for 315.4 Developmental Coordination Disorder

Performance in daily activities that require motor coordination is substantially below that expected given the person's chronological age and measured intelligence. This may be manifested by marked delays in achieving motor milestones (e.g., walking, crawling, sitting), dropping things, "clumsiness," poor performance in sports, or poor handwriting.

The disturbance in Criterion A significantly interferes with academic achievement or activities of daily living.

The disturbance is not due to a general medical condition (e.g., cerebral palsy, hemiplegia, or muscular dystrophy) and does not meet criteria for a Pervasive Developmental Disorder.

If Mental Retardation is present, the motor difficulties are in excess of those usually associated with it.

Coding note: If a general medical (e.g., neurological) condition or sensory deficit is present, code the condition on Axis III.

This definition is more remarkable for what it excludes rather than what it includes. It lists the essential features of the condition without attempting to list or even suggest what the other features may include. It limits diagnosis of the condition to those cases where 'the impairment significantly interferes with academic achievement or activities of daily living'. Most significantly, the definition makes no attempt to set out the causes of the condition, preferring instead to exclude a number of possible causes.

The variation in the symptoms from child to child has prompted a number of researchers to speculate that there may be a number of varieties of the condition, each focussing on a particular skill. The best distinction between types of dyspraxia as linked to the areas affected is found in Maureen Boon's book:

- verbal dyspraxia

- sensory integrative dysfunction

- ideational dyspraxia (difficulty in planning the best way to undertake a movement task)

- ideomotor dyspraxia (difficulty in converting planned movement into actual movement).

(Boon 2010, p.11)

Previously, she had also included:

- oral dyspraxia

- occulomotor dyspraxia (difficulty in coordinating vision and movement in a task)

- constructional dyspraxia (difficulty in building solutions)

- dressing dyspraxia.

(Boon 2002, p.12)

Several researchers have recognized that the causes and symptoms of dyspraxia vary and have attempted to differentiate between various types of the condition. Most have simply compared the results of a range of movement tests in order to find similarities and differences between children. Some have watched the children in order to identify differences and others have attempted to understand the causes of the children's problems and differentiate that way. This concept of identifying various types of dyspraxia may prove useful if it diminishes the expectation that a single universal cause and intervention may be discovered for dyspraxia and instead focusses attention onto several different causes that each require a separate intervention that needs to be identified.

This already complex situation is further complicated by the fact that at the same time that dyspraxia was being identified and investigated other researchers were looking into a range of conditions that they referred to as 'specific learning difficulties'. The term relates to problems identified in an educational setting usually in reading, writing, spelling and number work, sometimes called the 'developmental tasks' of the school-age child. They include:

dyslexia (difficulties with spelling and reading);

Asperger's Syndrome (difficulties making friends, seeing things literally);

dyspraxia (difficulties with ball skills, poor handwriting at speed, difficulty with dressing);

Attention Deficit Hyperactivity Disorder (difficulty concentrating when noisy, easily distracted, impulsive);

deficit of attention and motor perception (difficulty in paying attention and movement control);

dysgraphia (difficulty in writing);

dyscalculia (difficulty with sums).

(Kirby and Drew 2003, p.2)

Who gets dyspraxia?

It would be easy to write off children with dyspraxia as being stupid, but this is not the case. In fact, the reverse is true, and those with specific learning disorders are more likely to be of above average intelligence and their difficulties unexpected when their general intellectual ability is taken into account. It has also been noticed that those with a specific learning disorder are unlikely to suffer from only one of these conditions. There is a debate currently taking place within the scientific community as to whether these people are all suffering with the same condition of 'specific learning difficulties' that is manifested in a range of symptoms that vary from person to person, or whether each condition listed above has a separate cause and a separate list of symptoms.

The incidence of dyspraxia

Most researchers estimate the incidence of dyspraxia at between 5 and 10 per cent of the population with three times as many boys as girls affected. To put these numbers in perspective, this means that if the average class contains 32 children, there could be as many as four children with dyspraxia in the class. If the class is equally divided between boys and girls then one girl out of 16 is likely to have dyspraxia and three boys out of 16 are likely to have the condition.

Symptoms of dyspraxia

There are a range of symptoms for dyspraxia but none of them is essential for a diagnosis. The skills of those with the disorder may vary from hour to hour and from day to day, depending on their level of exhaustion and their ability to concentrate, making diagnosis difficult.

Anecdotal evidence suggests that the symptoms of dyspraxia start shortly after conception (Kirby and Drew 2003, p.19). Research (Kirby and Drew 2003, p.20) has shown that movement by the baby in the womb starts at six weeks and after that, mothers report that babies in the sixth week of pregnancy, who later experience movement difficulties in childhood, have been identified by their lack of movement in the womb at this time. This would therefore mean that these problems occur very early in our development, but this requires further research in order to confirm the facts. Some researchers (Brookes 2007a; Brookes 2007b) have attempted to include cases in which the symptoms have been said to develop later in life in their research into dyspraxia, but these are outside the usual definitions as they cannot be described as developmental. Such cases often have their basis in some traumatic event and as such probably have a different physiological basis – their inclusion could therefore confuse research into the causes and treatment of the condition.

The symptoms of dyspraxia diminish in both number and significance as the child grows up and continues to develop. Most children are able to achieve acceptable standards of performance in the key skills of walking, running and talking just within the 'normal' time span, although their performance never quite reaches the same level as that of the average child, and some symptoms persist into adolescence and even into adulthood. As well as continuing to develop, the child also learns coping strategies to deal with his or her difficulties, such as avoiding PE classes or growing up and leaving school so that he or she is not required to take part in sporting activities.

Tests for dyspraxia

Serious problems exist in designing a test for a condition in which the symptoms vary from child to child and from day to day and even from hour to hour and when no symptom is essential for the diagnosis of the condition, and where no cause of the condition has been accepted.

A number of tests have been designed in order to identify those children with movement skills problems. These include:

Denver Developmental Screening Test (Frankenburg and Dodds 1967; Frankenburg et al. 1990)

Bayley Scales of Infant Development (Bayley 1969)

Peabody Developmental Motor Scales (Folio and Fewell 2000)

Schedule of Growing Skills II (Bellman et al. 1996)

Purdue Perceptual Motor Survey (Roach and Kephart 1966)

Bruininks-Oseretsky Test of Motor Proficiency (Bruininks 1978)

Fundamental Movement Pattern Assessment Instrument (McClenaghan 1976; McClenaghan and Gallahue 1978; Gallahue and Ozmun 1995)

Developmental Sequence of Fundamental Motor Skills Inventory (Seefeldt and Haubenstricker 1976; Haubenstricker, Seefeldt, Fountain and Sapp 1981)

Test of Gross Motor Development (Ulrich 1985)

Ohio State University Scale of Intra-Gross Motor Assessment. (Loovis and Ersing 1976)

Basic Motor Ability Tests – Revised (Arnheim and Sinclair 1979)

Movement ABC Battery for Children (Henderson and Sugden 1992)

Pediatric Evaluation of Disability Inventory (PEDI) (Haley, Coster, Ludlow, Haltiwanger and Andrellos 1992)

The School Function Assessment (Coster, Deeney, Haltiwanger and Haley 1998)

Ecological Task Analysis (Davis and Burton 1991)

Examination of the Child with Minor Neurological Dysfunction (Touwen 1979)

Kinaesthetics and Sensitivity Test (Laszlo and Bairstow 1985)

The Abilities of Young Children Test (Griffiths 1970)

Southern California Sensory Integration Test (Ayres 1972)

(Kirby and Drew 2003, pp.57–58)

In the UK there is an almost universal acceptance of the Movement Assessment Battery for Children Test (usually abbreviated to the Movement ABC). The test was designed by two researchers (Henderson and Sugden) into education from the University of Leeds in 1992 and the following photographs show a little of how it works.

Manual dexterity (fine motor skills)

Shifting pegs by rows

This boy is moving pegs across the board. For this task, we test how well the children perform with both their dominant and non-dominant hands.

Threading nuts on bolt

Here the boy is threading three nuts onto a bolt. We give him two attempts at this.

Flower trail

For this task, the child is asked to draw between two lines. Our subject focusses intently on his drawing.

Figure 1.1: Movement ABC photo album

Ball skills (throw and catch)

Two-hand catch

Here we throw the ball against the wall and catch it.

Throwing bean bag into box

One of the tasks in our Movement ABC test is to throw a bean bag into a bin.

Dynamic Balance

Hopping in squares
One hop in each square. No more; no less.

Ball balance
'All I have to do is keep this tennis ball on top of this board? No problem.'

One-board balance
'WHOA!!!!' As is demonstrated in this picture, it is quite difficult to stand on one foot on this block for very long. Don't worry folks, no children were injured in the making of this picture.

In the United States of America there is an almost universal acceptance of the Bruininks-Oseretsky Test of Motor Proficiency (Bruininks 1978); other countries use other tests. A comparison of the
two named tests found significant differences in the results and a
correlation of only 0.80, indicating that neither was better than the
other, but rather that the best results were achieved by undertaking
both tests (Crawford, Wilson and Dewey 2001). Other researchers
compared the results generated by three popular methods of testing children's movement skills, the Test of Motor Proficiency, the
Test of Motor Impairment (TOMI) and the judgement of teachers
found that each procedure identified a different set of children as
poorly coordinated (Crawford *et al.* 2001; Keogh 1982; Sugden
and Wright 1998).

My discussions with those regularly performing assessments
of children referred to them by schools, due to their movement
skills difficulties, indicate that a number of problems exist with
the current testing arrangements. The cost of testing kits at around
£750/$1200 has meant that most counties in the UK and equivalent
regions in the USA have purchased just one kit, thereby limiting
the potential number of tests to be performed. This also generally
means that the kit remains with one assessor, thus reducing the
opportunity for other assessors to gain the necessary knowledge
and experience of using it. If the kit was cheaper then it should be
possible for counties to purchase more and train more assessors and
it might even be possible to encourage some schools to purchase
their own kits and train their own assessors, with the possibility of
universal screening taking place.

The limited availability of the testing kits, together with the
need for statutory assessments, means that assessors have to visit
schools for individual tests. Each assessment takes half a working
day to complete. On top of that, there is travelling time to the
school, time spent meeting and greeting colleagues and making
essential rooming arrangements and setting up and putting away
the testing equipment so each test takes a full working day to
complete. This limits testing to a maximum of five children per
week, and with other responsibilities taken into consideration,

usually fewer. Several authors (e.g. Kirby and Drew 2003) have indicated that a number of additional tests are required for a full diagnosis with one group of experienced researchers and authors recommending that the tests need to be repeated by class teachers, PE teachers, special educational specialists, speech and language therapists and others. They also suggest using the tests in a wide range of settings whilst the child uses reading, writing, speaking and other skills which will, of course, considerably extend the time taken to complete the diagnosis.

Another complication in assessing children suspected of having dyspraxia is that diagnosis tends to take place in two ways. When *teachers* identify a problem they refer the child to the school's special educational needs coordinator (SENCO) who will assess the child and then refer the child to an educational psychologist for a comprehensive assessment. If *parents* are troubled by their child's movement difficulties they will take the child to see their doctor. If the general practitioner is satisfied that there is a problem he or she will refer the child to a paediatric specialist at their local hospital.

These specialists possess widely different knowledge and experience and this will be reflected in their assessment of the condition. When a child is assessed by a doctor, he or she will generally accept anecdotal evidence of movement skills problems from the parent. The doctor will, however, have the clear ability to consider the incidence of any other medical condition which may be present and will devote all available time to considering this issue.

An educational psychologist conducting an assessment will generally undertake a full and careful assessment as set down in his or her training. An educational psychologist's ability to consider alternative medical diagnoses, must, of necessity, be limited when compared to that of the doctor.

In the UK a code of practice has been established for the assessment of children with movement skills difficulties. The code of practice provided for communication between parents and teachers, referral to school SENCOs and professional assessment by an educational psychologist. Unfortunately, as the code is a Department for Education document (2001), parents are generally unaware of it unless they communicate with a teacher and therefore many parents, identifying movement skills difficulties in their child, take him or her to see their doctor, who then makes a diagnosis in his or her own way.

Table 1.1: Process of assessment from Code of Practice for Special Educational Needs

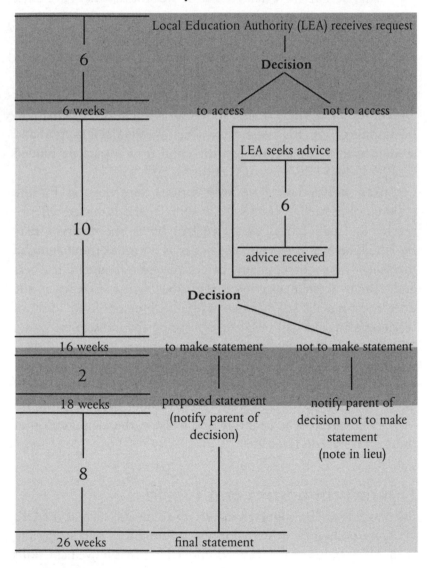

Department for Education (2001)

The teaching and medical professions have vastly different areas of knowledge and expertise and few doctors have the training, experience or equipment necessary to carry out a Movement ABC test on a child brought to them by a concerned parent.

The Movement ABC test is almost 20 years old. It is universally accepted in the United Kingdom as the official and best test for dyspraxia, despite the extensive list of weaknesses that have been revealed in the literature. Its greatest strength is that it allows children with movement difficulties to be assessed in a range of activities. This enables a trained and experienced assessor to identify the specific problems that underlie the difficulties that the child is experiencing and which have been identified by parents and/or teachers. The test also allows an element of objectivity to be introduced into the assessment, which is essential if support and assistance are to be provided to the child from a publicly funded service, such as Education or Health.

Errors in diagnosis have very serious consequences for the children concerned. A child with dyspraxia who is missed will not receive the support and assistance that he or she deserves, may be disciplined for accidents that occur as a result of undiagnosed movement difficulties and may be considered a failure by teachers and parents. A child diagnosed with dyspraxia, when he or she does not have it, will struggle with the pre-conceived ideas of teaching staff and will be given an excuse for indiscipline and a lifelong licence to under-perform.

There is a need for a quick, cheap, simple and objective test capable of providing reliable and valid results. Such a test would encourage further research into the condition, support efforts to identify an effective intervention and assist in the identification of those with the condition.

Dyspraxia across the world

Dyspraxia is only recognized in certain countries, such as the UK, USA, Australia and Western Europe. In countries still struggling with AIDS and HIV it is easy to understand that movement skills among children are not a priority. In countries where schools are held outside and without expensive technology, dyspraxia is less of a problem.

It should also be noted that the tests that form the Movement ABC test are sensitive to social, ethnic, gender and cultural factors which affect the results. The instructions accompanying the testing kit set down that the tests should not be of practised skills but rather of new activities outside of the child's experience – or raw skills. Indeed, the instructions generally call for the assessor to permit one practice attempt for each activity so as to allow the subject an opportunity to become familiar with the activity and the equipment.

One of the tests for a child aged between eight and ten years is the two-hand catch (see p.29). This requires the child to stand eight feet away from a flat wall and throw a tennis ball against the wall and catch it without allowing it to bounce or touch his or her arms or chest. Most boys born within the Indian sub-continent will score ten out of ten for this test and almost double what boys born in England or girls from the Indian sub-continent will score. This is surprising until one realizes that an Indian boy's cricket-obsessed father will probably have him practising this activity for several hours each week, thus distorting the result of this test and its reliability as a test of any innate skill. Another test is to thread three nuts onto a bolt in a timed exercise. Most boys brought up in England have some familiarity with nuts and bolts and experience little difficulty in this task. Many girls and boys from Third World countries have never seen nuts and bolts and repeatedly drop them on the floor, unable to understand why the nuts will not stick to the bolt for them in the same way that they did for the assessor when he or she was demonstrating the activity. There are a number of other similar examples.

As new tests were designed their details were published in peer-reviewed journals so as to permit the researchers to evaluate each others' findings and select the best test. Unfortunately, instead of agreeing on a common test, each country decided to use their own test, and where different tests are performed different results usually follow, leaving doubts as to the reliability and validity of the testing.

The Movement ABC test is widely used in Europe, Southeast Asia and Australia, although it is not as common in the United States where the Bruininks-Oseretsky Test of Motor Proficiency is widely used. Other tests are used in other countries.

Strengths of people with dyspraxia

It is interesting that only one author, Mary Colley, has related any positive effects from dyspraxia (Colley 2006). The theory that too many brain cells are produced, that they are then allocated to tasks and that the excess cells are destroyed during a child's development (Kirby and Drew 2003, p.18) would clearly indicate that a deficiency in one area was compensated by a strength in another area. It is also likely that having to deal with a problem is likely to develop a strength. It has been suggested that those with dyspraxia are 'creative, determined, original and hard-working' possessing 'strategic-thinking and problem-solving skills' (Colley 2006) and this might be explained by the constant need to invent excuses for knocking over the furniture, to try to stop doing it again and struggling to control movements to avoid the problem if all else fails. They can also be very caring and intuitive, whilst some have become gifted writers, such as Victoria Biggs, author of the book *Caged in Chaos* (2005).

The symptoms of dyspraxia have been shown to be quite diverse and the advice of a range of specialists may be required in order to assess problems and identify potential interventions. The following table shows some of the professionals it may be appropriate to consult, some of the qualifications and expertise that should be considered when seeking assistance, the services that these specialists should be able to provide and the best times to seek their assistance.

Table 1.2: Professionals involved in evaluation of children with developmental motor concerns

Professional	Typical services provided	Qualifications	When referral is indicated
Audiologist	Perform hearing tests Obtain hearing aids or other devices	Master's degree Clinical fellowship year (CFY) National certification exam	Delayed speech or language Parent concerns about hearing Recurrent ear infections
Developmental or behavioural optometrist	Assess eye health, acuity and functional vision skills Provide interventions that may include vision therapy to address problems with visual efficiency	Completion of a four-year graduate program leading to a Doctor of Optometry (OD) Completion of postgraduate examination by one of two organizations: 1. American Academy of Optometry or 2. College of Optometrists in Vision Development	Physical signs of eyestrain Poor reading comprehension despite good vocabulary and speech Blurred or double vision Frequently losing place during reading Avoidance of visual activities
Developmental paediatrician	Diagnosis and medical management of developmental delay	Board certified paediatrician Three-year fellowship in developmental paediatrics	Suspected developmental disorder Conflict of opinion regarding diagnosis or management of developmental concerns
Geneticist	Testing to determine presence of inherited diseases	Medical degree Fellowship and board certification in genetics	Congenital malformations or stigmata Family history of mental retardation, genetic disease, chromosome abnormality, known or suspected syndrome

Table 1.2: Professionals involved in evaluation of children with developmental motor concerns cont.

Professional	Typical services provided	Qualifications	When referral is indicated
Neurologist (paediatric)	Evaluation and management of nervous system disorders	Medical degree Residency in paediatric neurology Board certification	Loss or plateau of developmental skill Known or suspected seizures Unknown aetiology of developmental disability
Occupational therapist	Evaluation and management of problems performing daily living skills	**Occupational therapist:** BS or MS in occupational therapy Board certification Licensure (varies by state) Advanced paediatric certification available for paediatrics, sensory integration, or neurodevelopmental therapy **OT assistant (OTA):** AS in occupational therapy Board certification Licensure (varies by state) Must be supervised by occupational therapist	Limited ability to succeed in daily activities Limited mobility, especially fine motor Poorer nonverbal than verbal development Frustration leading to task avoidance, poor attention or problems with social interactions

Physical therapist	Evaluation and management of problems with mobility	**Physical therapist:** BS or MS in physical therapy Board certification Licensure (varies by state) Advanced paediatric certification available for paediatrics, sensory integration, or neurodevelopmental therapy **PT assistant (PTA):** AS in physical therapy Board certification Licensure (varies by state) Must be supervised by physical therapist	Delayed gross motor development or abnormal movement quality
Psychiatrist	Evaluation and management of emotional disorders	Medical degree Residency (paediatrics, internal medicine and/or psychiatry) Board certification	Suspected impairment in emotions or thought processes Serious behavioural or adjustment problems
Psychologist	Evaluation of cognitive capabilities and potential Measurement of academic achievement and educational needs Evaluation and management of problematic behaviour	**Psychologist:** Doctoral degree in psychology Internship and fellowship (varies by state) State licensure	Undiagnosed development delay Decline/regression in skill development School performance poorer than expected Inappropriate or atypical behaviour

Table 1.2: Professionals involved in evaluation of children with developmental motor concerns cont.

Professional	Typical services provided	Qualifications	When referral is indicated
		School psychologist: Master's degree in psychology Supervised field experience State licensure National certification exam (NCSP)	
Social worker	Provide support to child and family around social and emotional adjustment Assist family to identify and access community services or entitlements Design and implementation of specialized programs of educational instruction	Master's degree in social work Licensure (some states) Advanced certification available (ACSW) Minimum requirements: Bachelor's degree in education One semester supervised student teaching Certifications (e.g. early childhood, reading specialist): Varies by state	Suspected child abuse or neglect Acute distress in child or family Chronic stress related to care giving responsibilities Poor parental adjustment to diagnosis Assistance needed for referral, access or funding for services Child meets eligibility requirements as defined by state for early intervention or special education
Speech language pathologist	Evaluation and management of problems with communication	Master's degree in speech/language pathology Clinical fellowship year (CFY) National certification exam Licensure (some states)	Delay or impairment in communication skills Problems with oral-motor coordination affecting speech

(Kurtz 2008)

Summary

As a society we are confining our children to smaller and smaller classrooms containing more and more technical equipment. They are required to restrain themselves to prevent themselves from damaging valuable equipment and to control their movements tightly in order to use that equipment to best effect. Previous generations have been encouraged to run wild and expend their energy and the change has not suited every child.

This move inside has, it could be argued, resulted in the identification of a new condition, dyspraxia, that is not completely understood and for which no reliable test exists. It appears to be related to other similar conditions, such as dyslexia.

Currently support for children with dyspraxia revolves around a comprehensive assessment which attempts to identify the cause and symptoms for each individual child and leads to the development of a tailored program to assist that child. This is both time consuming and expensive in my view and another way needs to be found to tackle the problem.

Chapter 2

The Causes of Dyspraxia

Despite a considerable amount of research being undertaken by scientists from a wide variety of specialisms over the last 75 years, no definitive cause of dyspraxia has yet been established.

This is not surprising when you consider that the condition has such a wide variety of symptoms that vary from child to child and from hour to hour, depending on the individual child's state of health and level of exhaustion. With no single essential symptom necessary for diagnosis, testing is problematic and, as a result, research into the condition suffers.

Samuel T. Orton, the author of the first paper on movement difficulties in children (Orton 1937), was a consultant neurologist. He claimed that the condition that he had observed was likely to be caused by lesions of the brain. A lesion is 'any structural change in an organ or tissue resulting from injury or disease' (Collins English Dictionary). If this claim had been confirmed it would have identified the area of the brain requiring further study, but not the full mechanism of the disorder, nor the likely interventions needed to deal with the symptoms, as lesions have several causes.

Orton compared the observed symptoms of the disorder that he identified in children with the symptoms of an adult with an acquired apraxia in later life. He felt that a unilateral brain lesion affecting the dominant hemisphere of the brain would affect the highly skilled movements and language skills that he had observed to be troubling the children. This lesion would therefore reduce the movement skills on the dominant side of the body and reduce the affected person to a state of being 'doubly left-handed' as he described it.

The state of technology in the first half of the twentieth century did not allow for brain scanners of sufficient quality to verify Dr Orton's views and the condition was presumably not considered sufficiently serious to ethically justify surgery on an experimentally significant population of those with the condition. This meant that Dr Orton's views remained unconfirmed.

Since Orton's original paper, most scientists have discounted his views on the causes of movement disorders, choosing instead to believe that the condition is caused by a deficit of neural links, but lacking the scientific evidence to support their views. A neural circuit is 'a network of nerves and their interconnections' and the brain, like your computer at home, is constantly searching for shortcuts to speed up certain movements and processes. It is not known what prompts the creation of new neural links or how they are created, but they have a vital role.

Elite athletes, who train and practise skills for several hours a day for several years, often report that their best performances occurred when their actions became automatic and they did not have to think about what they were doing as they had practised so frequently. Athletes who have achieved some of the supreme performances in sport often have no memory of the event because the neural links had become so entrenched that the action had become automatic.

The second paper on children's movement difficulties was published in 1962 (British Medical Journal 1962). The author reviewed the published work of three sets of researchers into groups of local children experiencing movement difficulties, from Uppsala in Sweden, from Groningen in the Netherlands and from Newcastle-upon-Tyne in England. The author attended a conference on minimal cerebral palsy in Oxford and then linked all this to his own experience and research. He observed that the Swedish children were suffering from delayed development and that they appeared to catch up given time, accepted that the Dutch children's problems had been caused by anoxia (a lack of oxygen) and poor condition at and around the time of their birth and in the case of the English children specified that the disorder was not due to any disease or damage to the brain. After noting the similarities of the condition in the British children with those of children with lesions on the brain, he accepted this as the cause, thus supporting Samuel Orton's views on at least one cause of movement difficulties in children.

The conference attended by the author of the British Medical Journal article was organized by the National Spastic Society in Oxford, where consideration was given to the view that some clumsy children were afflicted with a form of minimal cerebral palsy and the author appears to have accepted that this might explain the symptoms of some children with movement difficulties.

The view that dyspraxia is a form of borderline or minimal cerebral palsy has been widely accepted by several subsequent authors (Hadders-Algra 2003) without any further research or comment. With both conditions sharing the same characteristic symptoms of abnormal muscle tone, reflexes, motor development and coordination, it is easy to understand this view. It is particularly interesting that the incidence of cerebral palsy has been strongly linked to anoxia at or about the time of birth or during pregnancy. Two of the four sources referred to in the BMJ article had suggested anoxia as a factor in the incidence of dyspraxia albeit one doing so indirectly.

It is now almost 50 years since the publication of the second research paper into children's movement skills. The two papers published between 1937 and 1962 identified a number of issues which appeared to the authors to be significant in the incidence of the observed movement difficulties in children:

- lesions on the brain
- a lack of neural links

- delayed development, from which children recover given time

- minimal cerebral palsy

- anoxia

- disorder not due to any disease or damage to the brain.

Recent research, using some of the latest technology, has confirmed most of these issues (Geuze 2007). Dyspraxia is not due to any disease or damage to the brain. Scanners are now able to identify the lesions on the brain which have been linked to the incidence of dyspraxia. Specialists still suspect that dyspraxia is linked to a lack of neural links, although there is currently no way of confirming their presence or absence or how they are formed. Dyspraxia is still seen as a developmental condition affecting movement skills in children, although it is recognized that the symptoms persist into adolescence and even adulthood unless suitable training to improve skills or coping strategies is developed. Anoxia, the lack of oxygen at or around the time of birth, with its links to dyspraxia and cerebral palsy is still seen as significant.

Support for the view that difficulties during pregnancy, particularly at or around the time of birth and quite possibly linked with anoxia, may be associated with movement disorders in children, came in 1992 when three scientists published research although no reason for them forming similar opinions at the same time has been identified. Birth trauma could cause the baby to be deprived of oxygen and therefore support the earlier research or it may be that the trauma is a symptom of the condition rather than a cause of it and further research is clearly required. Another researcher suggested that a large number of minor abnormalities, such as immature brain cells or congenital tumours, occurred during pre-natal development and that the body compensates for these problems by re-wiring around them and that this unique re-wiring may cause the difficulties experienced in movement skills (Farnham-Diggory 1992). Other research suggested that some children may have retained some primitive reflexes that cause shrugging, twitching, fidgeting and many of the symptoms of dyspraxia (Blythe 1992). This could have the effect of sending a signal intended for one limb to all four limbs so that they receive four times their anticipated number of messages, become confused and make mistakes. On occasion, not realizing that they have received an incorrect message, the limbs start to react before cancelling the movement, giving the impression of fidgeting.

Other factors linked by research to the incidence of dyspraxia include birth trauma, such as premature birth, precipitate birth, late delivery, forceps delivery, caesarean section, breech delivery, foetal anoxia and induced labour and mothers lacking essential omega oils during pregnancy.

Symptoms similar to those of dyspraxia have been identified in children whose mothers have consumed alcohol during pregnancy even in relatively insignificant amounts. This has been called Foetal Alcohol Syndrome, and there are a number of symptoms (McCreight 1997) but they are relatively minor and may appear insignificant when any movement difficulties are identified during an assessment of the child away from the presence of the mother many years after the children are born. Almost all social and recreational drugs are capable of crossing the placenta and causing death and congenital deformation of the baby (Pollard 2007). Little evidence exists as to whether these drugs can cause movement disorders, as research has focussed on the higher-end problems of causing death and congenital deformation rather than movement difficulties. The strength and nature of these substances suggests that there could be some connection, but this remains to be tested by scientific research.

The lack of a precise cause for dyspraxia has led to the American Psychiatric Association specifying unusually in their diagnostic criteria for the condition that 'the coordination difficulties are not due to a general medical condition' (American Psychiatric Association 2000). The full definition of dyspraxia in the manual is included in Chapter 1.

In the absence of a clear definition for dyspraxia, it is essential to have the best possible understanding of the causes of the disorder. Only in this way will it be possible to postulate the possibilities for preventing the disorder and the ways in which children with movement difficulties can best be helped. As the majority of books on the subject of dyspraxia have been written by educationalists and medical therapists, or are of the self-help variety, their authors are not qualified to comment on the causes of a condition which is generally accepted to be of a neurological nature and they have refrained from doing so.

Related research into the causes of dyslexia

Research into dyspraxia has failed to identify factors relating to the incidence of the condition and little other than speculation exists that may assist future research. In such circumstances the best solution may be a sideways glance at similar areas of study. Dyslexia is a specific learning disorder, like dyspraxia, and a great deal of research has been undertaken into the causes of the condition.

Whereas dyspraxia is often perceived as an 'inconvenience' in that children with the condition are a nuisance and knock over the furniture and disturb the classroom, dyslexia is a serious problem. Children who are unable to read have little place in the educational system, are unlikely to graduate or to take up employment that reflects their intellect, education, ability or ambition. Teachers look bad; success rates are lowered; questions are asked; something needs to be done. The serious nature of the condition is reflected in the amount of research that has been undertaken into it.

Children when reading require good skills to identify the characters and sound out the words that they see written on the page, but they also need the magnocellular area of the brain (see below) to be working efficiently to see what is written on the page. Those children with dyslexia appear to experience difficulties in the *magnocellular* part of the brain which measures time, distance and motion. It identifies and measures movements, including those of the head, which it is then able to balance out so that it effectively stabilizes images viewed by the child (Stein 2003). In dyslexic children that stability is lacking and the child's brain sees a blurred image on a page and in some cases may even see the words moving about on the page. These effects, separately and combined, make it very difficult for the child to read. It is very easy to understand how difficulties in the part of the brain that measures time, distance and motion could affect movement skills and cause children to suffer from dyspraxia. When the brains of those with dyslexia were compared with control brains, it was found that the magnocells in the dyslexic brains were 30 per cent smaller and significantly more disorganized than in the control brains. Consistent with this researchers recorded reduced and delayed averaged evoked potentials in response to a visual motion stimulus in alive dyslexics (Lehmkuhle and Williams 1993; Livingstone *et al.* 1991) although the results have been disputed (Victor *et al.* 1993).

Children with dyslexia also experience difficulties with their phonological skills that allow them to understand the sounds that certain letters and combinations of letters make. Phonological skills have no apparent effect on movement skills and will be passed over quickly here, but the fact that dyslexia is caused by a combination of two factors may assist in explaining the causes of dyspraxia and the reasons why it has proved so difficult to understand. The magnocellular system may be a factor in the incidence of dyspraxia but if it was the only factor then every child with dyslexia would also have dyspraxia. Phonological skills do not relate to movement skills and if they related to dyspraxia then similarly every child with dyslexia would also have dyspraxia. It would therefore be reasonable to assume that there is a second factor in the incidence of dyspraxia, but that it has not yet been identified. The fact that there are two factors and that both were required to be present for dyspraxia to occur would go some way to explain the difficulties that have been experienced in identifying the cause of dyspraxia.

There is a theory in neurodevelopmental science that during their normal development children produce more brain cells than they need. Later, as the child develops, between 15 and 85 per cent of the brain cells produced are destroyed by the body in a remodelling and rationalization process. The neuronal links between these brain cells will be lost at the same time as the cells themselves are destroyed. The theory proposes that although the final number of brain cells conforms to certain rules and varies little from child to child, the size of each functional area of the brain may vary at this time from child to child. (Kirby and Drew 2003, p.18). This apparently random process could clearly result in affected children being advantaged and disadvantaged in various abilities and functions and may explain a lack of magnocellular cells in certain children.

Summary

Research into the causes of dyspraxia remains at a very early stage. It has shown a link between the incidence of lesions in the brain and the incidence of dyspraxia and there is speculation that anoxia in pregnancy particularly at or around the time of birth and trauma at birth may be a factor – but there is little reliable research to support any of this. The similarities between dyslexia and dyspraxia appear to provide the strongest basis for finding a cause for the disorder, with a lack of fatty acids during pregnancy, and a reduction in the size and number of magnocellular cells requiring further investigation. None of this, however, suggests a viable intervention that could reduce the incidence or symptoms of the condition, other than fatty acid supplementation. It thus appears likely that the best intervention may have to come from methods designed to improve skills in the general population.

Recent technological advances have permitted the development of scanners capable of examining the human brain in sufficient detail to show lesions (structural changes in an organ or tissue resulting from injury or disease) on the brain that have been associated with the incidence of movement difficulties in children (Geuze 2007), but the exact mechanism of how these lesions result in the symptoms of dyspraxia has not been explained.

Chapter 3

The Importance of Exercise

But we do know what the Greeks knew: that intelligence and skill can only function at the peak of their capacity when the body is healthy and strong; that hardy spirits and tough minds usually inhabit sound bodies.

(President Kennedy 1960)

That which is used develops, and that which is not used wastes away.

(Hippocrates, fourth century BC)

Growth, maturation and development

From conception to the age of 19, children spend almost 20 years growing, maturing and developing. From an embryo a young man may grow to close to 2 metres tall and 100kg in bodyweight. His fitness will improve proportionately. From being unable even to roll away from a potential predator, he will be able to sprint 100 metres in as little as 10 seconds. This process of growth, maturation and development (and eventually degeneration) follows a pre-determined plan from conception to death.

Whilst each of us is an individual, affected by both nature and nurture, our development follows strict guidelines, so that doctors and physiologists are able to produce tables showing patterns of development, which can be used by health visitors, school nurses and parents concerned at a child's rate of development. Specialists can assess our children's growth, maturation and development and identify any problems at the first opportunity so that these may be investigated, diagnosed and, if necessary, treated, as quickly as possible. The areas covered in these tables may include:

- growth, such as height, weight, seated height, limb length and size of head
- physiological development, such as strength, endurance, fitness, speed, etc.
- development in movement skills and the ages at which these skills are achieved
- landmarks in speech and language skills
- cognitive and perceptual development
- perceptual and social skills.

Table 3.1 is an example of such a presentation of typical development.

Table 3.1: Milestones of typical development

Age	Fine motor	Gross motor	Speech language	Cognitive/perceptual	Perceptual/social
3 months	Hands remain open during rest	Head lags behind when pulled to sitting from lying on back	Coos/smiles in response to pleasant tones Laughs aloud Searches for sound with eyes	When lying on back, promptly looks at toy and follows with eyes	Shows anticipation of bottle/food through facial response
6 months	Passes toy from hand to hand when lying on back Rakes at tiny object using all fingers	Plays with feet while lying on back Rolls in both directions Sits with hands propped forward Stands and bounces when held by both hands	Pays attention to music or singing Understands "hi" and "bye-bye" Imitates familiar sounds, babbles (e.g. "wawa," "baba")	Shakes rattle on purpose	Holds own bottle Drinks from cup that is held by adult Mouths/gums hard cookie or cracker
9 months	Grasps block with fingers, not palm of hand Wrist is extended (bent back) during grasp of block	Head leads when pulled to sitting from lying on back Creeps or crawls on all fours Sits independently with hands free for play Pulls to stand at low table	Stops activity when name is called Understands "no" Uses some gesture language Participates in "pat-a-cake," "peek-a-boo"	Holds one block or toy in each hand and bangs together at midline	Feeds self cracker Finger feeds small bits of food (like cereal or cut-up vegetables)

Table 3.1: Milestones of typical development cont.

Age	Fine motor	Gross motor	Speech language	Cognitive/perceptual	Perceptual/social
12 months	Builds tower of two blocks Uses mature pinch grasp (thumb and tip of forefinger) Holds crayon using fisted grasp Helps to turn pages in a book	Stands alone without support Takes first steps	Responds to simple commands without any gestures Knows one body part Beginning to use single words meaningfully	Imitates scribbling with crayon	Brings pre-filled spoon to mouth, but spills Holds handle of cup while drinking Holds out arms and legs for dressing
15 months	Builds tower of three blocks Can place small pegs in pegboard	Crawling is discarded except on stairs Plays while squatting Gets to standing position without holding on to anything	Points to object when named Points to several body parts	Fills container with blocks Scribbles with crayon without demonstration	Shows awareness/discomfort when diaper is soiled Scoops food with spoon (spills)
18 months	Builds tower of four blocks Turns pages of book, two or three at a time	Seats self in small chair Climbs stairs holding rail	Refers to self by name Puts together two-word sentences	Inserts simple shapes into a formboard	Removes socks Sometimes indicates the need to eliminate before an accident Chews semi-solid food

	Fine Motor	Gross Motor	Language	Adaptive / Cognitive	Self-Help
24 months	Builds tower of seven blocks Strings small beads	Kicks a ball forward Jumps with both feet leaving floor	Produces 25–200 words Jargon has disappeared Points to pictures in book Enjoys listening to simple stories and nursery rhymes	Matches three colours Imitates strokes (circular scribble, straight vertical line) with crayon	Holds glass with two hands Has bladder control Imitates housework Drinks from straw Recognizes edible/nonedible food Helps pull down pants Finds armholes to pullover shirt
30 months	Builds tower of nine blocks Turns pages of book one at a time Shows preference for one hand	Climbs stairs with one foot to each step Stands on one foot briefly Rides tricycle	Understands taking turns	Imitates circle, horizontal stroke with crayon Names own drawings, even if unrecognizable	Uses napkin Unfastens large buttons Puts away jacket/toys Assists in pulling on socks
36 months	Builds tower of ten blocks Holds crayon with fingers like adult Cuts "fringe" with scissors	Runs on toes Runs, turning sharp corners without falling Performs broad jump about 12 inches' distance	Vocabulary of about 1000 words Carries on purposeful conversation No longer repeats or echoes others	Imitates cross with crayon Names and sorts objects by colour Counts three objects correctly	Feeds self with fork, spoon, rarely spilling Zips and unzips zipper once engaged Snaps front snaps Buttons large buttons Puts on shoes, wrong foot Turns water on/off

Table 3.1: Milestones of typical development cont.

Age	Fine motor	Gross motor	Speech language	Cognitive/perceptual	Perceptual/social
42 months	Can place ten pellets or raisins in small bottle within 25 seconds Shifts crayon up/down in fingers to adjust	Stands on tiptoe for ten seconds Hops on one foot		Names some letters and numbers	Puts shoes on correct feet Knows front from back of clothing Puts on mittens Can undo buckle Blows nose into tissue
4 years	Can place ten pellets or raisins in small bottle within 20 seconds Cuts 1-inch [2.5cm] wide line within half inch	Performs somersault Catches a beanbag with the hands (not against body) Performs broad jump about 24 inches [60cm] distance	Can recall four digits in sequence Speech is 90 per cent understandable	Copies square with crayon Draws one or two letters, numbers	Removes pullover garment Puts socks on correctly Washes/dries face/hands effectively Runs brush/comb through hair Places dirty clothes in hamper Sets table with help
5 years	Can place ten pellets or raisins in small bottle within 10 seconds Cuts out square within quarter inch	Runs through obstacle course avoiding obstacles Skips with alternating swing Stands on one foot for 10 seconds		Counts ten objects correctly Prints first name Draws recognizable face with eyes, nose, mouth	Drinks from water fountain without help Serves self and carries tray in line Wipes self after toileting Dresses without supervision Ties the half knot on shoes Looks both ways to cross street Bathes/showers when reminded

Age					
6 years	Can move coin from palm of band to fingers to place in soda machine	Performs one each of sit-up and knee push-up Rides two-wheeler	Likes silly stories and riddles	Copies triangle and crude diamond Prints all letters and numbers one to nine without a model to copy Prints last name Performs simple addition and subtraction Discriminates left from right	Uses knife/fork to eat Ties bow Closes fastener on back of clothes Cares for nose effectively Initiates phone calls to others Fastens back buttons Adjusts faucet temperature for bath
7 years			Reading and writing at school	Prints three to four word sentences Reversals in writing are no longer common	Styles hair Knows value of coins
8 years					Bathes/showers independently Remembers to wash ears Sweeps, mops or vacuums floors
10 years				Writes in cursive instead of printing	Ties necktie Uses stove or microwave independently Uses household cleaning agents appropriately Uses deodorant
12 years					Counts change for purchases costing more than $1 [~65p].

(Kurtz 2008, pp.18–22)

Factors in development

Development is directed by genetics. It has often been said that the most important decision that a child wanting to become an Olympic champion has to make is choosing his or her parents. By the time that the child has been born, many genetic factors have been fixed, although researchers investigating the human genome hope to be able to make changes to it in the near future. There are, however, a range of lifestyle factors that do influence growth, maturation and development. These include nutrition and exercise as well as ensuring adequate rest and relaxation, abstinence from cigarettes and alcohol and a secure home environment where excessive stress is avoided. This book will focus on three of the most important and most easily improved factors. It will comment briefly on nutrition and sleep, concentrate on exercise, and pass over the social issues.

Nutrition

Until the last 50 years, finding food of sufficient quality and quantity has been a problem throughout history for most people in the world. Only after the restrictions imposed by the Second World War were relaxed did improved transport links provide the food that most people needed. As soon as food was easily available at reasonable prices, industry began investigating processing technologies in order to make food more attractive but which increased sugar and salt levels and led to obesity. Obesity should not be a problem for young children who are supplied with an ideal, nutritionally balanced diet that will ensure for them a long and healthy life and be restrained from obtaining significant amounts of unsuitable, unhealthy food. Government programs are providing the training on nutrition that should prevent adults or children from being able to claim that they lack the knowledge to make informed decisions on what they eat.

Sleep

Growing children require approximately eight hours of sleep each night. There is an old saying that states that an hour of sleep before midnight is worth two after midnight and this certainly has an element of truth to it. Modern lifestyles tend to divert children from these guidelines. Many children have televisions, DVD players, computers and computer gaming machines in their bedrooms. These machines encourage children to stay up late and entertain them if they wake up during the night, so that instead of turning over and going back to sleep they stay awake and play. Many children take mobile telephones to bed with them and are then awoken by other children calling or texting them. All these machines are best left downstairs at night so that children can sleep undisturbed.

Exercise

There is now an almost universal acceptance that exercise is an essential factor in a healthy lifestyle. In adults, frequent and regular aerobic exercise has been shown to help prevent or treat serious, life-threatening conditions such as high blood pressure, heart disease, obesity, Type 2 diabetes, insomnia and depression (US Department of Health and Human Services 1999). Frequent and regular strength exercise contributes positively to improving muscle strength and joint mobility, maintaining a healthy bodyweight and building and maintaining healthy bone density (Baechle and Earle 2008). According to the World Health Organization, a lack of physical activity contributes to approximately 17 per cent of heart disease and diabetes, 12 per cent of falls in the elderly, and 10 per cent of breast cancer and colon cancer. In fact, exercise increases our physical fitness and, as part of a balanced exercise program, each of the sub-components of physical fitness including:

- strength
- endurance
- muscular endurance
- flexibility

- speed
- body composition.

There is also evidence that vigorous exercise (90–95% of VO2 Max (the amount of oxygen consumed during maximum exertion)) is more beneficial than moderate exercise (40 to 70% of VO2 Max). Some studies (Wislett, Ellingsen and Kemi 2009) have shown that vigorous exercise executed by healthy individuals can increase endorphins, and increase testosterone and growth hormone, effects that are not as fully realized with moderate exercise.

Not everyone benefits equally from exercise. There is tremendous variation in individual response to training: where most people will see a moderate increase in endurance from aerobic exercise, some individuals will as much as double their oxygen uptake, while others can never augment endurance (Bouchard *et al.* 1999). Similarly, only a minority of people will show significant muscle growth after prolonged weight training, while a larger fraction experience improvements in strength. This genetic variation in improvement from training is one of the key physiological differences between elite athletes and the larger population (Kolata 2002).

In children the physiological response to exercise is different from that in adults. For children, exercise is a developmental activity, essential to their physical, physiological, psychological, social and emotional growth. Playing increases their strength and fitness, encourages their hearts and lungs to develop, allows them to build self-image and self-confidence, learn to mix with their peers and deal with success and failure.

Children are generally healthy and do not as a rule suffer from the conditions resulting from a lack of exercise in adults, such as high blood pressure, heart disease, Type 2 diabetes, insomnia and depression, until much later in life, although we are starting to see a problem with children suffering from obesity. Whilst there is currently little scientific evidence that a lack of exercise immediately affects the health and fitness of our young people (Rowland 2007), it does, of course, build patterns of living that have been shown to cause the health problems associated with inactivity in later life.

A lack of exercise in childhood may eventually prove to cause the problems that occur in later life, making them worse than they would otherwise have been, but further long-term research will be required to confirm this.

Exercise in the past

Since the start of the Industrial Revolution in the late eighteenth century there have been doubts raised about the health and fitness of the younger generation. The movement away from an agricultural economy to an urban industrial economy reduced the reliance on manual labour by increasing the use of alternative forms of energy such as coal, steam and water, causing fundamental changes to a range of socio-economic and cultural factors and eventually to the lifestyles of all working people.

A number of authors have felt the need to go into print on this subject with two of those being worthy of special mention. First, Max Nordau published a book entitled *Degeneration* in 1892 and introduced his concept of 'fin de siècle' which he described as 'the dusk of the nations' and the 'autumn of human life' Nordau 1892, (pp.1–2) whereby degeneration would lead to the eventual decline and fall of the human race, explaining that the Industrial Revolution had led to large towns – more railways – more alcohol consumption – more food – less exercise, and – degeneration. The book was so successful that it had to be reprinted six times in the first year and is still in print today.

In 1899 Lieutenant-Colonel Robert Baden-Powell published a book entitled *Aids to Scouting* aimed at soldiers (Baden-Powell 1899). The next year he returned home, promoted to Major General and a popular hero after his success in defending the city during the Siege of Mafeking in the course of the Boer War. When he heard that the Director General of the War Office had issued a memorandum pointing out that between 40 and 60 per cent of those applying to enlist in the army were unfit for service, he was prompted to revise his book so that it addressed teenage boys and highlighted the need for outdoor physical activities, re-publish it as

Scouting for Boys (Baden-Powell 1908) and set up the International Scouting Movement, as Europe prepared for the First World War.

After the Second World War the restrictions that had been imposed on urban children in order to ensure their safety during the Blitz, and which had prevented them from playing in the streets, were lifted and they swiftly returned to spending their days running, jumping, playing football and climbing trees. From the 1950s onwards greater affluence, mass car ownership and modern housing estates combined with an increased perception of danger from paedophiles following a number of widely publicized cases persuaded parents that children could best be protected within the home, entertained by their new electronic toys of television and radio and later by videos, video games and computers and their successors.

Physical education

Physical education at school is generally failing to provide the exercise and hard work that our children need. Teachers of physical education (PE) are being restrained in the way that they deal with their students, for fear of provoking allegations of bullying. Requests for toilet and drinks breaks cannot be delayed however frequent and frivolous and requests for treatment of injuries cannot be denied however trivial the claimed injury. Few primary schools employ qualified PE teachers and as a result, those teaching PE restrict themselves to simple games and activities, which the children find unchallenging and do not enjoy. This causes the children to seek opportunities to escape from the lessons, by producing letters from parents exempting them from participation, by requesting toilet or drink breaks or by seeking attention for minor injuries, all of which their managers require the teachers to respond to positively. One school visited recently, a Sports College with responsibility for the local sports partnership, recorded just 11 per cent participation in PE classes during the year in question. In comparison with physical education lessons, children sent out to play unsupervised are naturally competitive and derive great pleasure from competing against their peers in any game or activity. No child ever sought permission to miss play through an injury.

The children become deeply involved in these games and activities and honestly lose all track of time. These children will last for exceptional periods of time without a drink break or a toilet break and with no adults handing out sympathy, see no point in reporting injuries and therefore carry on playing regardless.

Exercise and children with dyspraxia

Children between the ages of five and eight years develop their own perception of themselves and their place in society. They form views on their appearance, intelligence and abilities. Those who are unable to control their movements in class and who have become the butt of jokes for their 'clumsiness' and who are unable to impress with their skills in playground games will suffer in terms of self-esteem. They will seek ways of avoiding embarrassment, and these strategies usually include avoiding sport and games (Macintyre 2002), often claiming that they are 'too rough, boring or too tiring' (Geuze 2007, p.14).

Exercise is more important for those with dyspraxia. Several researchers have argued that *an active lifestyle is even more important for those who have disabilities* or disorders than for the general population. (Cooper *et al.* 1999; Steele *et al.* 1996; van der Ploeg *et al.* 2004). Their argument is based on the beneficial effects of exercise on the functional abilities of persons with disabilities or disorders. They also suggest that exercise reduces the risk of secondary conditions that are physical, medical, cognitive or emotional, or psycho-social consequences, and which a person with a primary disabling condition is predisposed to experience (Simeonsson, McMillen and Huntington 2002).

Child fitness levels

Exercise improves fitness and in order to understand why excercise has an important effect on dyspraxia it is necessary to look at children's fitness. Child fitness levels are the focus of a great deal of government attention, with almost daily reports in the national press relating to the latest scientific research and updates in government policy. Childhood obesity is recognized by the World Health

Organization (WHO) as one of the top ten problems facing us as we enter the twenty-first century (WHO 1992). Cardiovascular fitness levels among ten-year-old children are dropping at the rate of 4.8 per cent per decade (Sandercock *et al.* 2010). Sports coaches and PE teachers complain about the lack of movement skills of our children. Government advisors argue about which of these aspects of fitness should be given priority in their attempts to improve the health of the nation (BBC 2009). The health and wellbeing of our children is the cause of almost universal concern.

Obesity has benefited from considerable research (Berkey *et al.* 2000; Booth *et al.* 2001; Smith and Biddle 2008) and substantial efforts have been made to reduce the fatness of school-age children by taking statutory powers to close fast food restaurants near schools (*The Independent* 2009), by attempting to control school-time meals for their nutritional content and by improving labelling of the content of food supplied in restaurants and stores (FSA 2009). Governments are attempting to increase statutory provision of physical education for all children in an attempt to improve their fitness. Children's movement skills and the ways to improve them are now the subject of advanced study. Regrettably, little is being done to improve the children's movement skills, possibly due to a lack of knowledge and a focus on children's health, nutrition and diet in regular PE classes.

Strength

Strength has long been recognized as a factor in the incidence of dyspraxia (Platt 2010; Raynor 1989; Raynor 2001). Children who are weaker than their peers at school are more likely to have dyspraxia and the symptoms are likely to improve if they undertake strength training (Platt 2010; Raynor 1989; Raynor 2001). Strength is defined as 'the ability to generate maximum external force' (Zatsiorsky and Kraemer 2006, p.21).

With a definition discussing maximum external force and images of weightlifters breaking world records for the clean and jerk by holding 263 kg/580 lbs overhead and powerlifters breaking the world record for the squat with 457.5 kg/1007 lbs, it can be little surprise that strength is commonly associated with men with freakish muscles lifting outrageous weights. However, strength is clearly a measurable variable and whilst the champions are breaking their records some people lack the strength necessary to remain healthy and to perform the tasks of daily life. The National Strength and Conditioning Association (NSCA) of the USA has produced its *Basic Guidelines for the Resistance Training of Athletes* (Pearson *et al.* 2000) and the British Association of Sports and Exercise Sciences (BASES) its *Guidelines for Resistance Exercise in Young People* (Stratton *et al.* 2004). The two documents express similar views with the latter describing strength as 'essential for healthy living and the development of the healthy child' (pp.383–390).

It has long been recognized that one of the most frequent causes of injury is muscle imbalance, (Chandler *et al.* 1992; Croisier *et al.* 2002; Heiser *et al.* 1984), which is usually caused by a lack of strength in a muscle. This can occur at any age with some children emerging from the womb with muscle imbalances caused by awkward body positions whilst in the womb and with some older people degenerating and losing muscle strength unequally around the body. Treatment for all such injuries must include the strengthening of the muscle to eliminate the weakness that caused the injury or it will be likely to recur. This treatment will follow the same principles as all strength training whether designed to build weightlifting champions or to assist recovery following injury.

Everybody needs enough strength to live their life. A woman in her eighties requires the strength to perform a half squat with her bodyweight or she will be unable to rise from her armchair to make herself a cup of tea or to prepare a meal and if she is unable to do that she will be unable to live without support and assistance. The exercise program suggested by her physiotherapist will probably not involve tracksuits, leotards or metal weights but instead stress the need to keep getting out of the chair in order to strengthen the muscles of the legs and hips.

Physiotherapists are required to assist a substantial number of people with general or specific muscular weaknesses and most hospital physiotherapy departments contain multigyms, dynamometers (instruments designed to measure the force exerted by a muscle), medicine balls and sometimes even weight training bars, weights and dumbbells in order to assist them in this task.

Children with dyspraxia have been shown to have slack muscles and to lack muscle tone. They have been described as lacking in strength in their fingers, hands and wrists (Oliveira *et al.* 2006), which may relate to the difficulties that have been identified in completing a number of fine motor skills such as writing and drawing. Table 3.2 lists the physiological adaptations to resistance training and when these are compared with the symptoms of dyspraxia (see pp.19–20) it can be seen that these adaptations will benefit those children with dyspraxia.

Table 3.2: Physiological adaptations to resistance training	
Variable	**Resistance training adaptations**
Performance	
Muscular strength	Increases
Muscular endurance	Increases for high power output
Aerobic power	No change or increases slightly
Maximal rate of force production	Increases
Vertical jump	Ability increases
Anaerobic power	Increases
Sprint speed	Improves
Metabolic energy stores	
Stored ATP	Increases
Stored creatine phosphate	Increases
Stored glycogen	Increases
Stored triglycerides	May increase
Connective tissue	
Ligament strength	May increase
Tendon strength	May increase
Collagen content	May increase
Bone density	No change or increases
Body composition	
% body fat	Decreases
Fat-free mass	Increases

(Reprinted, with permission, from N.A. Ratamess 2008, p.96. 'Adaptations to anaerobic training programs.' In *Essentials of Strength Training and Conditioning*, 3rd ed., edited for the National Strength and Conditioning Association by T.R. Baechle and R.W. Earle (Champaign, IL: Human Kinetics), 96).

Recent research of mine assessed the strength of approximately 500 primary school children and compared it with the results of tests of fine and gross motor skills contained in the Movement ABC test used to identify cases of dyspraxia (Platt 2010).The results showed a clear and significant correlation between the children lacking in strength and those with movement difficulties. When the same children had completed a six week strength training program the tests were repeated and their results in the tests of fine and gross motor skills showed a clear and significant improvement.

These results confirm the work of Australian physiologist Annette Raynor (Raynor 1989; Raynor 2001) who revealed a link between dyspraxia and difficulties in muscle activation and co-activation (explained in Chapter 4). When these were improved through a strength training program, they combined to lead to improved neural control of movement. The results also confirm the results of the two superintendent physiotherapists, Lee and Smith (1998) mentioned in the first chapter, who found that an eight week strength training program, based on individualized observations of children with dyspraxia, produced a 72 per cent reduction in their symptoms. However, Lee and Smith's program was found to be too expensive to implement due to the time commitment required by specialist paediatric physiotherapists.

Lifetime motor development

Research has shown that human movement starts before we are born, early in pregnancy. As we saw in the introduction, there is anecdotal evidence from expectant mothers that those babies who experience movement difficulties in childhood may be identified by their lack of early movement in the womb, so movement difficulties may start very early in our development, but this requires further research to confirm (Kirby and Drew 2003).

Movement changes throughout our lives. Our bodies increase in length, girth, weight, proportion, muscle tone and strength as we develop in our youth and similarly these factors diminish in our declining years (Dick 2003). Our environment constantly changes, with changes in temperature, precipitation and lighting all affecting our perception. The objects with which we have to deal change in size, shape, velocity, changing our perspective and judgement.

> Every day, you move. This doesn't happen in a vacuum, though. Every movement you make occurs within the environment that surrounds you. You also move for a purpose – the tasks you perform have specific requirements. The way you move now has changed a great deal from your earliest movements, and will keep changing throughout your life. This is the essence of the study of motor development.
>
> *(Haywood and Getchell 2005, p.x)*

The fundamental nature of these effects is brought home to us by old age or by injury, when an assumed skill, learned half a century earlier, becomes impossible as a result of infirmity or a head injury. A task as simple as walking can become a problem when the surface on which we are walking changes.

> Our arms and legs move in different and distinct ways when we walk on a concrete sidewalk and when we walk on an icy sidewalk – or on a sandy beach. However, although the actual movements may differ, the motor skill we perform in each of these different situations is walking.
>
> *(Magill 2003, p.4)*

This quotation highlights the complexity of human movement and the importance of the calculations being made in the brain in order to walk from one surface to another, to move from concrete to sandy beach. If you read a biomechanics book you will discover the high level of mathematics involved in making these calculations. By the age of five, most children in the UK have started playing sports games such as football, cricket, netball or rounders. In football the players are required to run, dribble, pass, tackle, shoot and head the ball and interact with 21 other players, a ball and a referee. In cricket one has to be able to bat, bowl and field. Bowling requires you to run up and 'throw' a ball 22 yards so that it lands in the same small area every time. To field requires you to be able to run and catch a ball before it lands or chase it and stop it before it goes over the boundary. To bat requires you to assess the speed, direction, spin and movement in the air of a small ball coming towards you at great speed and strike it with a cricket bat. The levels of skill required in netball and rounders are broadly the same as football and cricket. In five years the child has made substantial progress in his or her movement skills. It is at about this time, as the child reaches five years of age, that parents and teachers start to notice the differing movement skills of children. As they begin to leave the family where they have been playing with siblings older and younger than themselves who may well possess similar movement skills, they go to school where they are compared to the other children in the area. This is the age when the most children with movement difficulties are sent for specialist movement assessment.

Individual difference factors that can contribute to differences in people's movement are:

- abilities

- attitudes

- body type

- cultural background

- emotional makeup

- fitness level

- learning style

- maturational level

- motivational level

- previous social experiences

- prior movement experiences.

(Reprinted, with permission, from Schmidt and Wrisberg 2008, p.163)

Human babies are born very small, very weak, out of proportion and unable to move in any controlled or planned manner. If they are to play organized games with their friends by the age of five they clearly need to grow taller, heavier and stronger and to learn a number of movement skills. If they want to continue to play games like football and cricket into secondary school they will have to maintain these skills at the same time as their bodies are changing in size, strength and proportion and as they are learning new, more advanced skills.

Landmarks of achievement in movement skills have been identified for babies and children until they reach the age of 12 years, which is about the average age at which they undergo puberty and reach young adulthood. The areas of achievement considered include:

fine motor control

gross motor control

speech language skills

cognitive/perceptual skills

perceptual/social skills.

(Kurtz 2008)

These landmarks are set out in full in Table 3.1. Tracking of a child's performance in movement skills against these landmarks permits an assessment of his or her movement skills.

We need to move in order to feed ourselves or to reproduce, to move away from predators or to find heat and cool, light and shade, friends and family and all those other things that we need or want. At birth we are small and unable to move in any way, even by rolling. We are totally dependent on our parents and require them to do everything for us. As soon as we are born we start to seek ways in which we can influence our environment. We learn that to cry brings an adult to attend to our needs. We learn that by gripping an adult's finger we can secure his or her complete attention. Movement starts to improve our situation.

Movement is a complex activity, requiring the coordination of physical and neural functions. From a purely physical aspect, it requires bones, lined with cartilage to reduce friction whilst moving, held together with ligaments, moved by muscles attached to the bones by tendons. Lack of muscle tone and weakness, particularly in the muscles of the hands and wrists has been shown to be a symptom of dyspraxia, as we have seen (Oliveira *et al.* 2006). No literature has been found that proposes or investigates any physical difficulties other than muscular strength, which may cause movement difficulties, in children and the possibilities are not pursued here. The neural functions which control movement are complex. According to Macintyre moving well involves:

> controlling the body as it moves
>
> coordinating different body parts so that movement is smooth
>
> gauging the correct amount of strength and speed
>
> understanding directionality
>
> being able to manipulate objects
>
> appreciating the rhythm of movements to aid repetition
>
> making safety decisions about when to move and where to move, and
>
> being able to stay still!
>
> *(Macintyre 2002, p.2)*

Summary

The perfect child has yet to be born. We each have defects and weaknesses that can be improved by exercise, training and experience of life. Good parents guide their child's development by arranging a healthy lifestyle and challenging developmental activities.

Physical development includes a range of activities ranging from endurance exercise that develops the heart and lungs to some form of gentle strength training. The success or failure of this work can be seen by comparing your child with their peers.

A lack of strength training will not only prevent your child from becoming a weightlifter, but will make any involvement in sport difficult. In the worst cases it may result in movement difficulties that cause them to go around home and school knocking over the furniture and result in relationship problems with their peers.

Chapter 4

The Basics of the Human Musculoskeletal System

The musculoskeletal system

In order to understand the reasons why the exercise program described in Chapter 6 works, it is necessary to understand a little about human movement and muscle activation and co-activation and in order to explain these terms it is necessary to revise the anatomy of bones, joints and muscles.

Figure 4.1: The human skeleton

The functions of bone and the skeletal system

The human skeleton consists of 216 bones, although this number may vary according to the method used to count them, as some of the bones fuse together as we mature and can therefore be counted as one fused bone or two separate bones.

Bones have the following functions:

1. *Support.* The skeleton provides a structural framework for the body by supporting soft tissues and providing points of attachment for most skeletal muscles.

2. *Protection*. The skeleton protects the most vital internal organs. For example, the skull protects the brain; the ribs protect the heart and lungs and the spine protects the spinal cord.

3. *Assisting in movement*. Most skeletal muscles are attached to bones and when the muscles contract they pull on the bones and produce movement.

4. *Mineral storage*. Several minerals are stored in bone tissue. These include calcium and phosphorus and when these minerals are required by the body they are released into the blood stream in order to maintain the supply and distribute the minerals to the parts of the body where they are required.

5. *Production of blood cells*. Red blood cells, white blood cells and platelets are produced in the red bone marrow of the larger bones in the body in a process called haemopoiesis.

6. *Triglyceride storage*. Yellow bone marrow consists mainly of adipose (fat) cells, which store triglycerides, which provide a potential chemical energy reserve.

Figure 4.2: Anatomy of a typical long bone

Joints

Joints are where two bones meet. The structure of each joint is different and the individual structure of the joint determines its combination of strength and flexibility so that joints that permit no movement are very strong and those that afford free movement are not as strong.

Muscles

Figure 4.3: Muscles of the human body (anterior view)

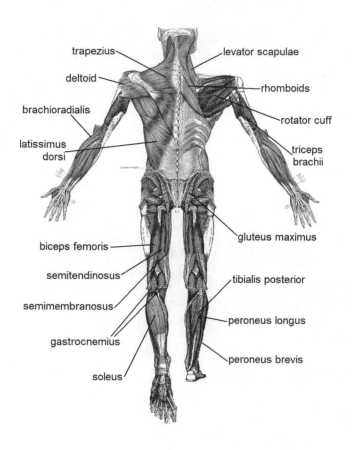

Figure 4.4: Muscles of the human body (posterior view)

Structure of muscle

Muscles are joined to bones, at both ends, by way of tendons. When muscles receive a signal from the brain to the motor neuron they contract and cause the bones, and therefore the body, to move. Fibres move in bundles, which turn on and off as they tire and run out of energy.

Figure 4.5: Anatomy of a typical muscle

Functions of muscle

Muscles work by contracting, maintaining a contraction and by relaxing and by combining these activities they are able to achieve the following five key functions.

1. *Producing body movements.* All body movements, including walking, running, writing or nodding the head rely on the coordinated functioning of skeletal muscles, bones and joints.

2. *Stabilizing body positions.* Skeletal muscle contractions stabilize joints and help to maintain body posture such as when we are standing or sitting. Postural muscles contract continuously when a person is awake; for example, sustained contractions of your neck muscles hold your head upright.

3. *Regulating organ volume.* Ring-like bands of smooth muscles called sphincters restrict the movement of contents of organs such as the bladder, the anus and the mouth by sustaining prolonged contractions. In the same way, temporary storage of food in the stomach or urine in the urinary bladder is possible because smooth muscle sphincters close off the outlets of these organs.

4. *Moving substances within the body.* Contractions of the cardiac muscle pump blood around the body through a system of blood vessels. Contraction and relaxation of smooth muscles in the walls of blood vessels assist to regulate blood flow by adjusting their diameter. In the same way, smooth muscle contractions also move food and other substances through the gastrointestinal tract, push gametes (sperm and oocytes) through the reproductive system, and propel urine through the urinary system. Skeletal muscle contractions aid the return of blood to the heart.

5. *Producing heat.* As muscular tissue contracts, it produces heat. Much of the heat released by muscles is used to maintain normal body temperature. Involuntary contractions of skeletal muscle, known as shivering, can help warm the body by greatly increasing the rate of heat production.

Muscle tissue

Muscle tissue constitutes about 40 to 50 per cent of the total bodyweight and is composed of highly specialized cells, including skeletal muscle tissue, cardiac muscle tissue and smooth muscle tissue.

Muscle work

Muscles work by contracting. They shorten to cause movement or they can create tension where movement is not possible because the resistance is greater than their ability to overcome it or they can relax and return to their natural resting length so as to allow other muscles to create movement or to allow gravity to create movement.

Skeletal muscles are attached to bones by way of tendons. Without tendons the rigidity of the bones would mean that the only part able to absorb the forces generated by violent movements, such as combat, would be the muscles, which would then be stretched and damaged. When muscles are attached to tendons, which are then attached to bones, the muscles produce movement by shortening and pulling on the tendons, which then pull on bones, causing movement. In this way the slightly elastic tendons protect the muscles from forces that could damage them.

Most skeletal muscles cross at least one joint and are attached to the bones that form the joint. When the muscle contracts it draws one bone toward the other, although the two bones do not usually move equally. The weight of the body usually means that the core of the body is held in its original position and a limb or other segment of the body moves towards or away from the core, depending on the action of the muscle. The end of the muscle which is closer to the core of the body is called the origin and the end further from the core of the body is called the insertion. The fleshy portion of the muscle in the middle of its length, between the tendons of the origin and insertion, is called the belly and contains the muscle fibres which contract to generate the force produced by the muscle. A good analogy is a spring on a door. The part of the spring attached to the door represents the insertion, the part attached to the frame is the origin, and the coils of the spring are the belly.

Group actions

Skeletal muscles are usually arranged in opposing pairs, so that there are flexors (benders) and extensors (straighteners), abductors (muscles pulling a limb away from the midline) and adductors (muscles pulling a limb towards the midline), and so on. A muscle that causes a desired action is referred to as the prime mover or agonist (= leader). Often, another muscle, called the antagonist (ant- = against), relaxes while the prime mover contracts. The antagonist has an effect opposite to that of the prime mover; that is, the antagonist stretches and yields to the movement of the prime mover. If the antagonist did not yield and both muscles worked at the same time then no movement would take place, although both sets of muscles would be working and would eventually reach exhaustion.

When you bend (flex) your elbow, the biceps brachii is the prime mover. While the biceps brachii is contracting, the triceps brachii, the antagonist, is relaxing in order to allow the bending to take place. Alternatively, when you straighten (extend) your elbow, the triceps brachii is the prime mover. While the triceps brachii is contracting, the biceps brachii, the antagonist, is relaxing in order to permit the arm to straighten. This example shows that the same muscle may be an agonist or an antagonist, depending on the movement, and is clearly set out in the figures below.

Figure 4.6: Bending the arm	*Figure 4.7: Straightening the arm*
The prime mover is the biceps brachii on the front of the upper arm. The antagonist is the triceps brachii on the back of the upper arm.	The prime mover is the triceps brachii on the back of the upper arm. The antagonist is the biceps brachii on the front of the upper arm.

Do not assume, however, that the biceps brachii is always the prime mover and the triceps brachii is always the antagonist. For example, when straightening (extending) the elbow, the triceps brachii serves as the prime mover and the biceps brachii functions as the antagonist. Most movements also involve muscles acting as synergists (SIN-er-gists; syn- = together; erg- = work), which help the prime mover function more efficiently by reducing unnecessary or unwanted movements. A good example of this is catching a tennis ball. The muscles of the hand also cross the wrist, so they also act on the wrist joint. When the fingers close to catch the ball the same muscles will bend the wrist, which would cause you to drop the ball, so the muscle which extends the wrist acts at the same time and this co-activation of the muscles that bend the wrist and the muscles which extend the wrist cancel each other out so that the fingers can grasp the ball without the wrist bending and we can catch the ball.

The movement shown from Figure 4.8 to Figure 4.9 is the desired movement, that of catching the ball:

Figure 4.8: Catching – open hand stage	*Figure 4.9: Catching – closed hand stage*
If we put our hand up to catch a ball, we usually start with our hand open and the muscles of our fingers and hand relaxed ready to catch the ball.	When the ball comes to hand we want the muscles of the fingers and the front of the hand to contract to catch the ball and secure it in our hand.

The movement shown from Figure 4.10 to Figure 4.12 is the actual movement produced when the muscles on the front of the fingers, hand and wrist contract, and result in dropping the ball:

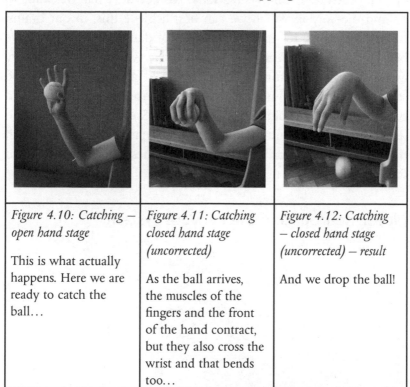

Figure 4.10: Catching — open hand stage	Figure 4.11: Catching closed hand stage (uncorrected)	Figure 4.12: Catching — closed hand stage (uncorrected) — result
This is what actually happens. Here we are ready to catch the ball…	As the ball arrives, the muscles of the fingers and the front of the hand contract, but they also cross the wrist and that bends too…	And we drop the ball!

Luckily, muscles can also work as fixators. This means that they operate to stabilize a joint by acting equally and opposite to another muscle in order to cancel it out. In this case the muscle at the back of the wrist acts to eliminate the unwanted portion of the movement, that of bending the wrist, so that we can contract the muscles of the fingers and hand to catch the ball, without also bending the wrist and dropping it.

Under different conditions and depending on the movement, many muscles act at various times as prime movers, antagonists, synergists or fixators.

Motor control

There needs to be a system in place to control and coordinate all our movements. In most situations, we decide what we want to do and the way in which we can best achieve this, in our brains. In rare situations, for example in cases of danger, our bodies have been programmed to make reflex actions, which are involuntary motor responses to stimuli. An example of a reflex is that if you stick your hand out into a flame, you will instantly pull the hand back in order to avoid burning yourself. So as to avoid wasting time which could result in injury the body has learned to deal with this reaction as a reflex without sending a message to the brain and thinking about what needs to be done.

Motor neurons and the nervous system

Figure 4.13: The human nervous system (Widmaier, E., Raff, H. and Strang, K. et al. (1990) Human Physiology. New Castle, DE: McGraw-Hill, p.168) Reproduced with permission of The McGraw-Hill Companies.

For a skeletal muscle fibre to contract, it must be stimulated by an electrical signal from the brain, transmitted down the spine, called a muscle action potential delivered by its neuron called a motor neuron. A single motor neuron along with all the muscle fibres it stimulates is called a motor unit.

Stimulation of one motor neuron causes all the muscle fibres in that motor unit to contract at the same time. Muscles that control small, precise movements, such as the muscles that move the eyes, have 10 to 20 muscle fibres per motor unit. Muscles of the body that are responsible for large, powerful movements, such as the biceps brachii in the arm and gastrocnemius in the leg, have as many as 2000 to 3000 muscle fibres in some motor units. As the axon (long process) of a motor neuron enters a skeletal muscle, it divides into branches called axon terminals that approach – but do not touch – the sarcolemma of a muscle fibre.

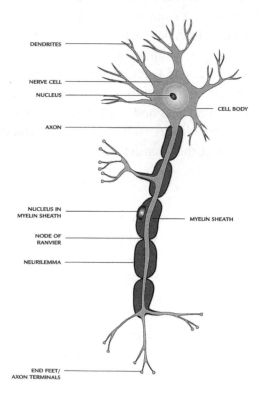

Figure 4.14: The structure of a nerve cell (Tucker 2002, p.76)

Activation and co-activation

Activation is the creation of tension in a muscle.

Co-activation is when the prime mover and antagonist both create tension with equal force so that there is no movement, as in an isometric contraction.

Conditions affecting the neural control of muscles

Some of the most serious conditions affecting the neural control of movement are listed below.

Poliomyelitis

This is often called polio or infantile paralysis, is an acute viral infectious disease spread from person to person. Although around 90 per cent of polio infections cause no symptoms at all, affected individuals can exhibit a range of symptoms if the virus enters the blood stream. In about 1 per cent of cases the virus enters the central nervous system, infecting and destroying motor neurons, leading to muscle weakness and acute flaccid paralysis. Polio has caused widespread epidemics to become one of the most dreaded childhood diseases of the twentieth century.

Epilepsy

Epilepsy is a common chronic neurological disorder characterized by recurrent unprovoked seizures that cause random muscle activations. These seizures are transient symptoms of abnormal, excessive or synchronous neuronal activity in the brain. About 50 million people worldwide have epilepsy, with young children or people over the age of 65 years the most likely sufferers; however, it can occur at any time. Epilepsy cannot be cured but is usually controlled with medication, although surgery may be considered in difficult cases.

Cerebral palsy (CP)

This is caused by damage to the motor control centres of the developing brain and can occur during pregnancy, during childbirth or after birth up to about age three. Cerebral palsy describes a group of permanent disorders of the development of movement and posture, causing activity limitation, that are attributed to non-progressive disturbances that occurred in the developing foetal or infant brain. The motor disorders of cerebral palsy are often accompanied by disturbances of sensation, perception, cognition, communication and behaviour, by epilepsy, and by secondary musculoskeletal problems. There is no known cure, although improvements in movement skills have been detected in some people with the condition who undertake strength training (personal conversation with David Kaye, National Weightlifting Coach for Cerebal Palsy Athletes).

Muscle fibre recruitment

When the brain wants a muscle to work, it sends an electrical stimulus down the spine and across the nervous system to the motor neuron, which controls the muscle. The muscle fibre requires a minimum amount of stimulation, called the threshold, in order to elicit a response. If the stimulation is less than this threshold, no muscle action occurs, but with any stimulation equal to or exceeding the threshold, maximal action occurs in the muscle fibre. This is known as the all-or-none response. Muscles consist of bunches of muscle fibres and because all the muscle fibres in a single motor unit receive the same neural stimulation all the fibres in the motor unit act maximally any time the threshold is met. Thus, the motor unit also exhibits an all-or-none response. Activating more muscle fibres produces more force. When little force is needed, only a few motor units are stimulated to act.

Until recently, scientists believed that there were two types of muscle fibres, fast twitch (FT) and slow twitch (ST). Fast twitch had a good supply of blood and were used in fast activities such as sprinting or explosive lifting. In diagrams they were shown in red. Slow twitch had a lesser supply of blood and were used in slower activities, usually requiring more endurance. In diagrams they were usually shown in white. Scientists have now discovered that there is a third type of muscle fibre, known as fast twitch type B (FT_b). These are muscle fibres that can switch between fast and slow twitch depending on the type of activities being undertaken over the long term. For example if the person is regularly sprinting the fast twitch type B fibres will act as simple fast twitch fibres; if the person is undertaking regular endurance work then the fast twitch type B fibres can switch to slow twitch to assist with the endurance work. As a result of this discovery, the 'ordinary' fast twitch muscles are now abbreviated to FT_a.

FT_a and FT_b motor units contain more muscle fibres than ST motor units. Skeletal muscle action involves selective recruitment of ST or FT muscle fibres, depending on the requirements of the activity being performed. In the early 1970s researchers demonstrated that this *orderly recruitment* is determined not by the speed of action but by the level of force demanded of the muscle.

Orderly recruitment of muscle fibres and the size principle

Most researchers agree that motor units are generally activated on the basis of a fixed order of fibre recruitment. This is known as the principle of *orderly recruitment*, in which the motor units within a given muscle appear to be ranked. Let's use the biceps brachii as an example. Assume a total of 200 motor units, which are ranked on a scale from 1 to 200. For an extremely fine muscle action requiring very little force production, the motor unit ranked number 1 would be recruited. As the requirements for force production increase, numbers 2, 3, 4 and so on would be recruited, up to a maximal muscle action that would activate 50 per cent to 70 per cent of the motor units. For the production of a given force, the same motor units are recruited each time.

A mechanism that may partially explain the principle of orderly recruitment is the size principle, which states that the order of recruitment of motor units is directly related to their motor neuron size. Motor units with smaller motor neurons will be recruited first. Because the ST motor units have smaller motor neurons, they are the first units recruited in graded movement (going from very low to very high rates of force production). The FT motor units then are recruited as the force needed to perform the movement increases. Some questions remain about how the size principle relates to most athletic movements because it has been examined only in graded movements that represent muscle actions of less than 25 per cent relative intensity.

However, even during maximal efforts, the nervous system does not recruit 100 per cent of the available fibres. Despite your desire to produce more force, only a fraction of your muscle fibres are stimulated at any specific time. This prevents damage to your muscles and tendons. If you could contract all the fibres in your muscle at the same instant, the force generated would likely tear the muscle or its tendon.

During events that last several hours, you must exercise at a sub-maximal pace, and the tension in your muscles is relatively low. As a result, the nervous system tends to recruit those muscle fibres best adapted to endurance activity: the ST and some FT fibres. As the exercise continues, these fibres become depleted of their primary fuel supply (glycogen), and the nervous system must recruit more FT_a fibres to maintain muscle tension. Finally, when the ST and FT_a fibres become exhausted, the FT_b fibres may be recruited to continue exercising.

This may explain why fatigue seems to come in stages during events such as the marathon, a 42km (26.2 mile) run. It also may explain why it takes great conscious effort to maintain a given pace near the finish of the event. This conscious effort results in the activation of muscle fibres that are not easily recruited. Such information is of practical importance to our understanding of the specific requirements of training and performance.

Motor units give all-or-none responses. For a unit to be recruited into activity, the motor nerve impulse must meet or exceed the threshold. When this occurs, all muscle fibres in the motor unit act maximally. If the threshold is not met, no fibres in that unit act. Activating more motor units and thus more muscle fibres produces more force.

In low-intensity activity, most muscle force is generated by ST fibres. As the intensity increases, FT_a fibres are recruited, and at the higher intensities, the FT_b fibres are activated. The same pattern of recruitment is followed during events of long duration.

The more than 600 skeletal muscles in the body vary widely in size, shape and use. Every coordinated movement requires the application of muscle force. This is accomplished by agonists, or prime movers, muscles primarily responsible for the movement; antagonists, muscles that oppose the prime movers; and synergists, muscles that assist the prime movers.

The smooth flexion of the elbow requires shortening of the brachialis and biceps brachii muscles (agonists) and relaxation of the triceps brachii (antagonist). The brachioradialis muscle (synergist) assists the brachialis and biceps brachii in their flexion of the joint.

The agonists produce most of the force needed for any particular movement. The muscles act on the bones to which they are attached, pulling them toward each other. Synergists assist this action and sometimes are involved in fine-tuning the direction of movement. The antagonists play a protective role. Think of the quadriceps (front) and hamstrings (back) in your thigh. When your hamstrings (agonists) contract forcefully, your quadriceps (antagonists) also contract slightly, opposing the motion of the hamstrings. This prevents overstretching of your quadriceps by the strong contraction of the hamstrings and allows more controlled thigh movement. This opposing action between agonists and antagonists also produces muscle tone.

Mechanisms of gains in muscle strength

Men who lift weights tend to get large muscles and, as few women lifted weights before 1980, it was assumed at that time that muscles got stronger by getting bigger. The fact that when limbs were damaged and immobilized in a plaster cast the muscles tended to wither, lose tone and become weak confirmed this belief. After 1980, when women and children started to lift weights, it was noticed that they achieved similar results to the men, but without the same increases in muscle bulk and it soon became clear that strength gains do not necessarily require increases in muscle bulk in order to occur.

Muscle size is not insignificant as a factor in strength and this is reflected in the need for weight classes in weightlifting and powerlifting in order to ensure fair competition and the fact that world records generally increase in each heavier weight class, but other factors, such as neural control, also play a role in increasing strength.

Neural control of strength gains

An important neural component explains at least some of the strength gains that result from resistance training. Enoka (1994) has made a convincing argument that strength gains can be achieved without structural changes in muscle but not without neural adaptations. Thus, strength is not solely a property of the muscle. Rather, it is a property of the motor system. Motor unit recruitment is quite important to strength gains. It may well explain most, if not all, strength gains that occur in the absence of hypertrophy, as well as episodic superhuman feats of strength.

Synchronization and recruitment of additional motor units

Motor units are generally recruited individually or in groups; they are not all called upon at the same instant. They are controlled by a number of different neurons that can transmit either excitatory or inhibitory impulses. Whether the muscle fibres contract or stay relaxed depends on the summation of the many impulses received by that motor unit at any one time. The motor unit is activated and its muscle fibres contract only when the incoming excitatory impulses exceed the inhibitory impulses and threshold is met.

Strength gains may result from changes in the connections between motor neurons located in the spinal cord, allowing motor units to act more synchronously, facilitating contraction and increasing the muscle's ability to generate force. There is good evidence to support increased motor-unit synchronization with resistance training (Raynor 1989; Raynor 2001), but there is still controversy as to whether synchronization of motor unit activation produces a more forceful contraction. It is clear, however, that synchronization does improve the rate of force development and the capability to exert steady forces.

An alternate possibility is simply that more motor units are recruited to perform the given task, independent of whether these motor units act in unison. Such improvement in recruitment patterns could result from an increase in neural drive to a muscle during maximal contraction. Although the results from several studies support this theory (Raynor 1989; Raynor 2001), others do not. It is also possible that inhibitory impulses are reduced, allowing more motor units to be activated, which is discussed further in the next section.

However, not all scientists agree that you can increase motor unit recruitment. Some believe that the scientific evidence indicates that all motor units are recruited even in the untrained state. Unfortunately, the research techniques available to study this issue are indirect, and thus not precise, which could explain some of the confusion about motor unit recruitment.

Summary

In summary, muscles are like light switches; they are either switched on or switched off. They are switched off until they receive an electrical signal from the brain and then they are switched on and shorten with all their strength, pulling the two bones to which they are attached closer together until the electronic signal stops. This switching on is called 'activation'.

Muscles perform a very simple task. These simple tasks are combined and coordinated by the brain to allow the human body to perform complex gymnastic movements. This is extremely complex and does not add to this subject, so will not be dealt with here.

Training to improve the muscles increases strength and improves the efficiency of the way that the muscles work. This program is designed to eliminate weakness and by so doing to reduce the movement difficulties experienced by some children.

Part II

The Exercise Program

Chapter 5

Why It Works

"What doesn't kill you makes you stronger"
(paraphrased by Nietzsche 1888)

Introduction

In previous chapters it has been shown that in the last century children have participated in less exercise and that their fitness and movement skills have deteriorated as a result.

Modern exercise programs

Patterns of physical activity in young children have also changed fundamentally in the last century (Washington *et al.* 2001). Self-determined and self-regulated free play (Schraw, Crippen and Hartley 2006) has almost completely disappeared due to a range of social, cultural and lifestyle changes that have taken place during this period. Only a belief, largely unsupported by scientific evidence, that the health and fitness of our young people will be affected by a lack of exercise (Rowland 2007) and the need for healthy recruits to the armed forces, has stemmed the decline. Parents, keen to ensure the health and fitness of their children, are arranging for them to participate in competitive sports (Washington *et al.* 2001) such as football, rugby, basketball and martial arts, where they will be protected, encouraged and coached by trained and approved professional staff. Simultaneously, as we have seen, the levels of fitness and the quality of the movement skills of our young people have troubled commentators (Baden-Powell 1908; British Medical Journal 1962; Nordau 1892).

It is widely recognized that free play by children allows for the development of motor skills (Piaget 1962 in Rowland 2007; Washington *et al.* 2001). Children need to learn a range of key movement skills in their early years, including throwing, catching, kicking and hitting a ball. These skills need to be learned at definite stages of each child's development and do not develop sooner simply as a result of introducing them to children at an earlier age (Branta *et al.* 1984 in Washington *et al.* 2001). They have traditionally been learned whilst participating in free play with the lessons reinforced during school physical education classes. Unfortunately, the reduction in time spent on free play has coincided with school physical education programs diminishing in duration and content (Washington *et al.* 2001) and as no competitive sport includes all of these skills, the skills are deteriorating. It is also necessary to consider the motivational factors acting on the children in play.

The informal nature of free play arouses many of the positive factors of variety, freedom and fun and permits a focus on success without the need to acknowledge failure. The more formal competitive sports must include a certain amount of regimentation and competition that can lead to acknowledgement of failure and embarrassment and, with poor coaching, can lead to boredom and injury.

There are few similarities between free play and competitive sport. Children can engage in free play at any time including that time before their parents get up and when they are at work. Historically, children went out after breakfast and were told to return for their evening meal. In order to participate in organized, competitive sport, facilities have to be hired and professional coaches paid, so sessions are likely to be limited to just one or two hours. In free play children keep going until their exhaustion overtakes their enthusiasm, whilst in competitive sport professional coaches encourage and even enforce regular breaks. Free play involves a wide variety of activities partly due to its duration and anecdotal evidence suggests that it often included wrestling, lifting, throwing and climbing. These are not popular competitive sports, and participation in them is likely to have diminished and if this is the case then the strength of the children is likely to diminish also.

Replacing free play with competitive sport is likely to introduce a number of other changes relating to the nature of the particular sport selected. The *frequency* of each session is likely to be restricted if adult coaches have to be paid at an hourly rate. The *intensity* of each session is likely to be restricted by cautious adult coaches. The *time* that each session is likely to last is likely to be restricted if adult coaches have to be paid at an hourly rate. The *type* of training is likely to be decided by the parents who arrange for the child to attend or by the adult coach supervising the session in the case of general sessions. Frequency, intensity, time and type combine to form the FITT principle used to assess the effectiveness of fitness training (Walker 2004).

Fitness in young people

The result of this caution is the reduction in the fitness levels of our children that is the focus of a great deal of government attention.

The government response was to set a minimum of two hours' participation in high-quality physical education for all children in 2002, and to announce in 2007 an additional £100m campaign to give every child the opportunity to participate in five hours of sport every week, but time for physical education and sport is only a small part of the solution.

Children today are overweight, lacking in strength and endurance and do not possess the movement skills of their ancestors. Their life expectancy, quality of life, health, education and fitness are all doomed to suffer as a result. It is a frightening prospect and one that is currently prompting a great deal of government action and investment, mainly focussed on increasing children's level of activity.

The solution

In comparison with physical education lessons, children sent out to play unsupervised are naturally competitive and derive great pleasure from competing against their peers in any game or activity.

The solution is to combine the features of physical education with the principles of unsupervised play, to produce what will be referred to here as 'feral play'. It is supervised with a light hand, involves all the principles of competition that motivates children, is great fun and improves strength and endurance explosively. Involving vigorous exercise as it does, it may even improve body composition and movement skills.

When these rules were applied by a sports coach during recent research they clearly excited the class teachers with the opportunities to help the children make real progress with their fitness and skills, but they also caused them a degree of professional embarrassment (senior managers in schools demand strict discipline and silence and it is now recognized that this severely inhibits children so as to restrict their performance and improvement in sport and PE) and it was eventually agreed that the classes would be run by the sports coach with the assistance of the class learning support assistant. However, many members of staff, several of them specialist PE staff, observed that the children looked forward to the lessons, exerted themselves strenuously during the lessons and upon their return to class told stories of their experiences in the classes. Many of the children asked when the classes would re-start. During informal conversations, members of staff have reported that the children's behaviour showed a marked improvement following these classes, once they had settled down after the excitement of the class. At least one of the schools which participated in the research has changed its policy in relation to the reporting for accidents, as a result of staff experience during the research.

In order to formalize the definition of 'feral play' and to encourage teachers and sports leaders at schools to experiment with it, the following guidelines have been produced:

Feral play

Feral play refers to the way that children used to amuse themselves in decades gone by. It relates to the uncontrolled, unrestrained way in which children used to play when let out of the house to meet up with friends and only return in time for their evening meal.

Feral play is physical, competitive activity. No breaks are taken for refreshment, drinks, toilet or even injury. It requires, and develops great strength, endurance, fitness, coordination, movement skills and self-confidence.

In its natural form, feral play does not involve adults, but the involvement of adults does not, in itself, prevent feral play from taking place, provided that the adult involvement does not become authoritarian, intrusive or break any of the other rules.

1. Supervised feral play should be limited to 30 minute sessions and start with a drink and use of the toilet, so that later requests for breaks may be safely declined.

2. The usual safety requirement for the environment, the equipment and the athletes (injury and dress) to be checked can be observed before the children arrive.

3. Simple safety rules, such as 'no go areas', are rigidly enforced. This may involve gymnasium equipment, etc. These should be kept to a minimum and may develop over time. Breach requires a short exclusion, maybe two minutes.

4. Any violence, physical confrontation, breach of the rules or cheating requires a warning before a short exclusion, maybe two minutes, if repeated.

5. The adult should imitate a rugby union referee as closely as possible, by constantly giving out instructions and naming offenders and giving personal instructions in order to gain compliance.

6. All unnecessary limits and restraints are avoided.

7. All injuries are ignored for one minute. Without attention most children will be keen to resume the activity. A little blood or a bruise or a sting will be forgotten in the heat of the moment.

8. All activities are based on competition and competition is encouraged as a positive activity.

9. The adult must be enthusiastic, relaxed and possess a long and varied list of challenging activities.

10. All sessions must end with a drink and use of the toilet, as no breaks will have been permitted during the session.

Progressive resistance training

The value of progressive resistance training in developing a healthy body has long been recognized by young men all over the world. According to Greek mythology, Milo of Croton (a wrestler from the sixth century BC) trained by lifting and carrying a newborn calf on his back every day. After two years the calf had become a cow and Milo had become a weightlifter (Pomeroy *et al.* 2009). Irrespective of the veracity of the story, it vividly sets out the principles and value of progressive resistance training. Soon a number of scientists became interested in the subject of strength training. Hippocrates (460–370 BC), the father of modern medicine, recommended it to his patients (Pomeroy *et al.* 2009). Another Greek, Galen of Pergamum (AD 129–199), who was given the position of personal physician to several emperors and whose theories dominated and influenced Western medical science for well over a millennium, recommended strength training exercises using an early form of dumbbell called halteres (Pomeroy *et al.* 2009).

The application of the principles of progressive resistance training in strength training programs has continued to increase through the ages. In 1955, Oscar State and Geoff Dyson published a book entitled *Weight Training for Athletics* (State 1955). It introduced the concept of weight training to the wide variety of running, jumping and throwing events in athletics in order to improve performance. This book started an expansion in strength training in sport that culminated in 1988 in the East German Olympic Committee announcing a policy that required athletes from every Olympic sport except sailing to undertake a program of progressive resistance training. In 1996 the United States Olympic Committee published a similar policy.

Traditionally, the lifting of heavy weights has had a reputation for being dangerous and unhealthy (Department of Education and Science 1980; Rugby Football Union 1990). Weights are excellent tools for promoting substantial physiological changes to the human body such as improved strength and increased muscle bulk, but accidents can occur when weights are not secured to bars and when weights are used without spotters. However, whilst the lifting of heavy weights clearly creates the potential for serious accidents to occur, records show that relatively few accidents actually occur and that relatively few people are injured in weights rooms so that weightlifting is one of the safest sports (Hamill 1994; Zatsiorski and Kraemer 2006). Weights rooms are like physiotherapy departments in that they contain much of the same equipment: bars, disks, collars, dumbbells, multigyms and medicine balls. The recognition of the potential risks and the enforcement of strict discipline in both the physiotherapy department and the weights room, ranging from dress codes to rules governing personal behaviour and the use of the equipment, have eliminated the risks.

Historically the use of weights by women and young men has provoked considerable debate. It has been said that women will grow bigger and more muscled and that young men will injure their epiphyseal plates and stunt their growth (Zatsiorsky and Kraemer 2006) and lose flexibility and become musclebound (Stratton *et al.* 2004). There is now an almost universal acceptance amongst sports scientists and medical staff that resistance training is safe for all ages and both genders and that all the identified risks from lifting weights can be resolved by high quality professional coaching. A number of high profile, respected bodies have published policy statements on resistance training for young people which confirm these views (Behm *et al.* 2008; Faigenbaum *et al.* 1996; Stratton *et al.* 2004). Several of the leading authors on strength training have now published books promoting the subject (Faigenbaum and Westcott 2000; Kraemer and Fleck 1993). It is interesting to note that the person voted the best weightlifter of the twentieth century and the first person to clean and jerk three times his bodyweight was a 16-year-old boy. Naim Suleymanov won Olympic Gold

Medals in 1988, 1992 and 1996, when he was refereed by the author of this book.

The science of strength training

The scientific principles upon which strength training is founded are simple and basic but for completeness and in recognition that not all readers will have a sports science background they are set out below:

- strength
- endurance
- fitness
- speed
- flexibility
- body composition.

The components are very closely related and this relationship is illustrated below:

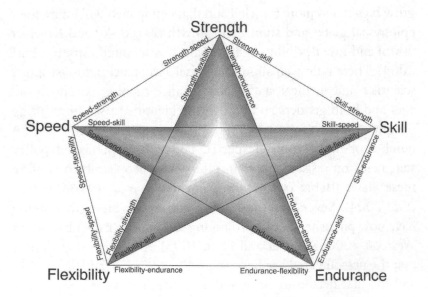

Figure 5.1: The relationship between the components of fitness (Stone, Stone and Sands 2007, p.4)

The Principles of Training (the principles on which all sports training must be based if progress is to be made) state that in order to improve fitness, all training must be

- progressive
- overload
- varied
- planned
- specific
- reversible.

All strength training programs must follow these principles in order to increase strength in any person.

Chapter 6

The Exercises and Session Plans

The sessions that we are proposing are designed to improve fitness and strength in the same way that children would improve their fitness and strength if left to play unsupervised with their friends.

'Fitness' is the ability to recover after a training load. It is important because it helps to develop the heart and lungs.

'Strength' is the ability to lift heavy objects or to overcome a resistance.

These sessions are not designed to build great strength, but rather to eliminate exceptional weakness and ensure that children with dyspraxia are no weaker than their average classmates. Research has shown that children with dyspraxia are weaker than their peers. (Raynor 1989; Raynor 2001) This weakness has been shown to be due in part to the fact that children with dyspraxia do not have the same ability as their peers to activate their muscles efficiently and because sometimes they coactivate, which means that they activate the muscles in pairs, so that they activate the muscles that straighten the leg at the same time as activating the muscles that bend the leg, so that these muscles cancel each other out (Platt 2010).

Equipment

These sessions have been designed so that almost no equipment is necessary to run them. A piece of flat, level ground approximately 20 metres (60 feet) long is ideal. Take off your jumpers to mark the strip that you are going to use. This marks your territory and means carrying less equipment. The only other equipment that is needed is a bench or log about 25cm (10 inches) high and stable, that can be used to jump on and off. If you cannot find something suitable take your time as the first few sessions can be an easy introduction whilst you find the bench or log. A tennis and/or squash ball is useful if you have one as this will help to improve the child's grip.

If the weather permits it is always nicer to exercise outside, where there is fresh air and a chance to commune with nature, although the presence of large, aggressive dogs and too many observers should be avoided, particularly at the start.

Clothing

Remember that children with dyspraxia are reluctant to take part in physical activity and it may be better, at least when starting the program, not to make a big deal out of getting changed into a fancy tracksuit and trainers. It may be better to keep to some old clothes that permit free movement and that you will not be worried to see get dirty or even torn. If these clothes are put on a couple of hours before the planned session it makes less of a deal of going training and children can go as they are and therefore be more relaxed about the session.

Shoes

Suitable footwear is more important than clothing, but nowadays most children consider trainers to be fashion accessories rather than sports equipment. Firm support and good grip are essential for running, jumping and hopping, which all put the foot under a little pressure. Again these can be put on a couple of hours before the session, so that going training is no big deal.

Changing

As the children become more used to participating in these sessions then it may be easier to get changed at the venue. Make sure that the children always have a good drink of water and always use the toilet. Remember that children with dyspraxia do not like taking part in physical activity and that they know that repeated requests to use the toilet or to get a drink will break up the session. As the session is only half an hour, there should be absolutely no toilet or drinks breaks. No healthy child needs to drink more than once in half an hour and they will drink at the start and at the finish of the session. Similarly, no healthy child needs to use the toilet more than once in half an hour and they will be encouraged to use the toilet at the start and finish of the session.

Gently encourage your child to ignore an injury that you did not see happen and for which you can see no consequences. Children enjoy the attention that they receive from you if they report an injury, however minor. Children have low pain thresholds and if something really hurts no amount of gentle encouragement will compel them to continue. You must then make a point of seeking them out 60 seconds later to ask how the injury feels. By this time most children will have forgotten the injury and be happy to continue. If they are not, treat the injury.

Supervision

Remember that you are responsible for all aspects of your child's safety. You should check that area that you propose to use for any broken glass, thorns or nettles, and so forth. Check any equipment that you propose to use during the session. Check your child for injuries and illnesses and that they are wearing suitable clothing and footwear. Make sure that you have a basic first aid kit for any little cuts, bruises or stings. Take a suitable sunscreen along if working outside.

The exercises

Running

This is a simple activity, familiar to all children. There is no need to focus on the technique unless you feel that there is a serious problem with it.

Figure 6.1: Running

Hopping

Another simple activity, familiar to all children. This adds variety to the session and keeps the children thinking as well as exercising. Hop right foot up the track and hop left foot back down the track.

Figure 6.2: Hopping

Jumping

Put two feet together and jump along the track. Some children find it a little difficult to keep their feet together whilst jumping to start with, but they all pick it up very quickly if given time. Vary this exercise by making each jump as long as you can or by touching the ground with both hands between jumps. These variations make the child work their legs a little harder.

Figure 6.3: Jumping

Figure 6.4: Jumping and touching the floor

Bench stepping

Stand on top of the bench. Jump down onto the ground, with one foot either side of the bench. Jump up onto the bench again. Repeat this 20 times.

Stand on top of the bench.	Jump down onto the ground, with one foot either side of the bench.	Jump up onto the bench again.

Figure 6.5: Bench stepping

Bench jumping

Repeat this exercise ten times at a good pace.

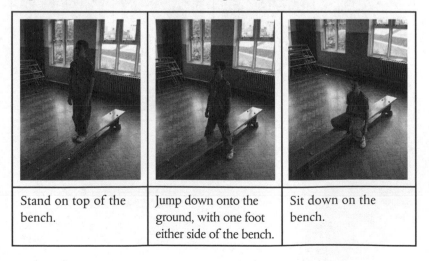

Stand on top of the bench.	Jump down onto the ground, with one foot either side of the bench.	Sit down on the bench.

Figure 6.6: Bench jumping

Crush the ball

Repeat this exercise ten times.

Pass the ball to the other hand and crush it as tight as you can ten times.

Hold the ball in the palm of one hand.	Crush it as tight as you can.	Bend your wrist towards you to finish.	Relax your wrist.	Open your hand.

Figure 6.7: Crush the ball

Children with dyspraxia have been found to have weak fingers, hands and wrists that may result in them experiencing difficulties in fine motor skills such as writing and drawing.

Session plan

Session 1

20 metre (60 foot) relays

1. 1 × running

2. 1 × right foot hopping

3. 1 × left foot hopping

4. 1 × bunny hopping with two feet together

5. 1 × bunny hopping touching the ground between hops.

6. 1 × sprint race

4 × 10 each hand crushing the tennis ball.

Session 2

Bench straddle jumps (stand on the bench, jump down onto the floor straddling the bench, sit on the bench, and then jump back on the bench).

Repetitions = Week Number × 4

Repetitions = Week Number × 6

Repetitions = Week Number × 10

Repetitions = Week Number × 15

Repetitions = Week Number × 20

How often?

During their summer holidays, primary school children will play all day every day, if allowed to. I would recommend that they be allowed to participate in this program six days a week. This will allow them one day each week in order to recover from their exertions. By the time the children move to secondary school they can no longer manage to exercise six days and three or four days would be more appropriate.

How long?

Each session should last 30 minutes from the time that they start exercising until the time that they finish. As far as possible, there should be no breaks and no distractions during this time. Toilet breaks and drink breaks occur before and after the session and no healthy child needs to go for either more than every 30 minutes.

How intense is the session?

Primary school children can run continuously for well over an hour, so 30 minutes should be no problem for them. Let them go at their own pace, with sensible encouragement from you. Be careful not to drive them harder than they want to go. When you get a chance, go to a local park and watch children in self-directed play without parental intervention. The children work ten times harder than their PE teachers ask them to at school.

Recovery

After exercise, an athlete needs to complete three stages of recovery. The first is to re-hydrate, which is best achieved by taking sips of cool water from a bottle. Be careful not to drink too much too quickly or to drink ice cold water if you are warm after exercise. The second stage is to re-energize and this is best achieved with a piece of fruit or a handful of dried fruit. The third stage of recovery is to clear the lactic acid, which is the waste product from burning up all the energy during exercise. This is best done with a long warm shower, followed by a brisk rub down with a nice, rough towel.

Summary

A simple exercise program has been set down and explained that will bring the weaker child back to the level of strength of his or her peers. This should improve the efficiency of children's muscles so that they improve their movement skills to the level of the other children in their class.

Being a strengthening program, it is of short duration, but dynamic and vigorous.

Chapter 7

What You Can Do to Support a Child During the Exercises

Safety

This book is about helping children to overcome a difficulty that they are experiencing. Parents and teachers are essential to achieving the goals of the session but they should try to play down their involvement as much as possible.

The primary purpose of the parent or guardian is to protect the children. A session in which you bring back the same number of children that you take, and avoid a stop off at the local hospital even if the children don't get to exercise, is a better one than the session where the children achieve all their exercise goals but just one child gets injured or lost.

Avoid becoming involved in the details of the session and keep focussed on the overall strategic picture of what is going on. The success of the session does not depend on you setting out the cones as there are children around who would be flattered to be asked to help you to set them out. Stand in the middle of the park and direct operations and make sure that the cones are put where you need them to be.

From your position in the middle of the park you can see all the children and you can see any that are drifting away from you as well as anybody who is approaching the group. Keep counting the children every couple of minutes. It is very easy to keep a watchful eye over a group of children and to take pleasure over how well everything is going and then realize that you haven't seen little Johnny for half an hour.

You will only have control of what is happening if everybody can hear you. There is a modern view that volume is not important in coaching sport, but the children cannot do what you want them to do if they don't know what you want them to do. If you don't want to shout, then take a whistle.

There will need to be enough adults for the number of children that you are taking. Whilst one adult can control 30 children in a classroom, the number is far less without those walls to restrain the children. Remember that children cannot simply be allowed to go off on their own to the toilet or to get a drink, so there will need to be adults available to supervise these activities.

Remember that the law requires checks to be made on adults working with children to ensure their suitability to do so.

Be aware of any adults that get close to the group and act to prevent them getting too close or too involved with your children.

The 'trick' is to anticipate any problems as early as possible and to act promptly to remove any risks or threats. The longer you fail to act, then the worse the situation is likely to get. You don't usually have to take dramatic action, but don't ignore situations.

Your venue

Visit your venue and have a look around before you arrange to take half the children in the neighbourhood down there. Perhaps, take your own children with you. Let them run around. If they find the potholes and the dog poo this time it will save a lot of problems next time.

Take a piece of paper and a pencil with you. Draw a map of the site and illustrate the local toilets, the coffee shop and such places. Mark the car park and how far it is to walk to the spot that you have chosen. The map doesn't have to be a work of art as long as you can read it and understand it.

Mark a point where parents or ambulances can meet you in case of emergency. Practise explaining to an emergency operator where you want the ambulance sent because next time a child might be bleeding when you have to do this. A useful tip is to select a rendezvous point which is close at hand and easily found by the ambulance crew who may not know the area. Remember that most fields don't have street names and numbers and asking the ambulance crew to find the third oak tree on the left may leave you waiting a long time for them to find you.

Equipment

As any parent will tell you, even the simplest activity session requires you to take a considerable amount of equipment.

It is difficult to justify not taking a first aid kit with you when you are taking other people's children to play in a park. A few plasters and a couple of dressings are better than nothing. A qualified first aider is ideal, but confidence in your ability to deal with simple cuts and bruises is essential.

A mobile telephone allows you to call for help if things go wrong and you need the police to chase off troublesome youth or the ambulance service to take a child who fell onto broken glass to hospital. Check that the telephone works where you are going. You will need signal, battery strength and credit for it to work. Sometimes a mobile telephone will work on one side of a football pitch, but not on the other side, and it is not good policy to wait until you need to use it to find out where it works. Do not allow yourself to become distracted by answering calls yourself, however important they may seem at the time. Your task now is looking after the children.

A list of the names of the children and the contact numbers of their parents or guardians allows you to summon adults to take troublesome children home or to inform the relatives of injured children. The more numbers that you have the better and the more up to date they are the better. You will never realize the value of this list until something goes wrong!

Although some parents may be reluctant to supply you with a medical history of their child for the first session, if you are taking the same children regularly then you may like to find out any who have conditions that could cause you problems, such as diabetes, epilepsy and asthma. As long as you are aware of the children with these conditions then you can familiarize yourself with the treatment and what the parent wants you to do should the child need help. (Johnny has a little blue inhaler in his pocket and two puffs are usually enough; a carbonated drink usually puts him right, etc.)

As previously stated, nobody can follow your instructions if they can't hear them. If you cannot shout loud enough or don't like to do so, then you will need a whistle and everybody will need to know what you want them to do when you blow it. The simplest system is for everybody to stop and look at me when I blow the whistle and I will give you a hand signal of what I want you to do. Alternatively, one blow means stop, two blows mean…

Plastic cones allow you to mark out the area that you are using for the session. Nobody leaves this area without your permission. Remember as the person in charge you must be able to say where every child is at every minute. Cones can be almost as valuable as the walls in a classroom if properly used.

You will need to take food and drink along to the session. A bottle of fresh water is required for very hot days and is useful for washing lumps of mud out of cuts. Keep a non-return valve on the top of the bottle if possible. You may well find that one or two of the children are diabetic and may need calories urgently if exercising. This is not a problem as long as you can give them something. Cans of carbonated drinks are ideal for this purpose. You can open them, tip some away and then shake the contents to dispose of the gas and then you are left with a very sugary drink that is ideal for diabetics. Sugar lumps, glucose lumps or candy bars are also useful. Chocolate is good but can get very messy on sunny or warm days.

Remain calm

This chapter has set out a number of steps that need to be taken in order to avoid problems that may occur and to deal with any that do occur. You should not allow this to intimidate you or deter you from the plans that you have set down. These are simple precautions to avoid things that can go wrong and most can be achieved in a few minutes. Hopefully, you will organize these sessions for years and never have any problems, but it would be stupid not to prepare for the worst.

On the day

Develop a positive mental attitude: this is going to be fun! Fun for my child. Fun for the other children. Fun for me.

Try to be available well before the session is due to start, so that you are relaxed and not rushing. Have everything ready so that nothing can go wrong. Read through your checklist one more time.

Checklist

- Check the times that the park is open.

- Check the times that you and your child are available.

- Give eight hours' notice of the session to your child so that he or she can prepare him- or herself.

- Ensure that your child is suitably dressed for the session well before it is time to go, so that the session is no big deal.

- Make sure that your child has suitable trainers or footwear on well before it is time to go.

- Ensure that you have a piece of fruit or a handful of dried fruit and a bottle of water for your child when he or she finishes training.

- Make sure that you have a session plan for the session. If you keep a book in the car with a record of previous sessions then a brief note can be made after the sessions and minor adjustments made for next time.

- Take a change of clothing in case of rain.

- Have fun and get home as soon as possible.

- Remember that you are here because your child experiences difficulties in doing this.

- Do not expect world records. Acknowledge every achievement. Praise him or her frequently.

It is about taking your children down to the park to play. The task should be fun for both parent and child; a chance for some one-to-one time.

If you have other children, then arrange the sessions to take place when somebody else can look after them. You are there to focus on the child with dyspraxia and to help him or her overcome his or her problem. No good at all will come from trying to take two or three children to the park at the same time. You cannot focus on two or three children at the same time and the sessions will have no value.

If either of you feel that this is a burden then the sessions will soon stop. Neither of you will want to spend time under pressure and under stress. Make the sessions short, sharp and fun. Don't let it drag out into an hour or two by adding games of football and so on. Arrange other trips to the park for that. Let this session be fast, enjoyable and then go home.

Do not worry about trying to become a sports coach in order to help your child to perform better. It is not necessary.

You should start to notice an improvement in your child's movement skills by the end of the sixth week and the best improvements will then come over the next six weeks.

The principles that govern the session are the principles of good parenting.

For those parents who are new to coaching sport, it may be useful to consider what we are trying to achieve, what the children may expect and work out a philosophy for our work and for this reason the Bill of Rights and key points are included.

Bill Of Rights for Young Athletes

- Right to participate in sports

- Right to participate at a level commensurate with each child's maturity and ability

- Right to have qualified adult leadership

- Right to play as a child and not as an adult

- Right of children to share in the leadership and decision-making of their sport participation

- Right to participate in safe and healthy environments

- Right to proper preparation for participation in sports

- Right to an equal opportunity to strive for success

- Right to be treated with dignity

- Right to have fun in sports.

(Reprinted, with permission, from Martens, R., Christina, R.W., Harvey J.S., and Sharkey B.J. (1981), *Coaching Young Athletes* Champaign, IL: Human Kinetics, p.7

Key points to remember

Athletes are motivated to play sports to fulfill their need for fun and to feel worthy.

People have a need for an optimal amount of arousal.

When optimally aroused, the 'flow experience' is more likely to occur.

You can help athletes experience optimal arousal and thus flow by fitting the difficulty of the skill to the ability of the athlete, keeping practices varied and all players active, and avoiding continually instructing and evaluating your athletes.

Sports are potentially threatening to young athletes because they equate their achievement with their self-worth.

Success-oriented athletes see winning as a consequence of their ability, blaming failure on insufficient effort.

Failure-oriented athletes attribute losing to a lack of ability and infrequent wins to luck, thus blaming themselves for losing and yet not taking credit for winning.

Failure-oriented athletes attempt to protect their self-worth by putting forth only token effort so others will not discover their feared lack of ability. Coaches often mistake this lack of effort as a lack of motivation, but in actuality, failure-oriented athletes are highly motivated to avoid the threat to their self-worth.

Coaches develop expectancies of athletes which, when conveyed, may become self-fulfilling prophesies.

Failure-oriented athletes are most vulnerable to coaches' negative expectancies.

Athletes learn to fear failure because:

a. a. the mistakes and errors that are a natural part of the learning process are misinterpreted as failures;

b. competitive pressures result in youngsters setting unrealistically high goals which assure failure; and

c. athletes begin playing for extrinsic rewards rather than to attain personal goals.

The most important thing you can do to enhance your athletes' motivation is to teach them that success means achieving their personal performance goals rather than the performance goals of others.

You can play a vital role in helping athletes to set realistic goals. Realistic goals are those that motivate athletes to achieve their finest but to recognize their limitations as well.

Athletes perform best when they are optimally aroused or motivated. Too little or too much arousal impairs performance.

Optimal arousal differs from skill to skill and from athlete to athlete.

Athletes become anxious when they are uncertain about whether they can meet the demands placed on them when meeting these demands is important to them. The greater the uncertainty and the more important the outcome, the greater the anxiety.

You can help alleviate athletes' anxiety by decreasing uncertainty and helping to reduce the importance of the outcome.

(Reprinted, with permission, from Martens, R., Christina, R.W., Harvey J.S., and Sharkey B.J. (1981), *Coaching Young Athletes* Champaign, IL: Human Kinetics, p.62

The role of the parent

Two good friends of the author, who are very experienced international coaches working with young children in gymnastics, have focussed specifically on 'the role of the parent'. Their comments are valuable and are reproduced here.

Children need their own unique support structure of immediate family, social environment and school. They may also need someone involved in their chosen interest (which in our case is physical activity) to stimulate their senses during formative years. Together, such a collection of potential supporters will undoubtedly best serve the needs of the child. As the 'line managers' of their offspring, it is the parents who are expected to take the lead in forming such a team, and undoubtedly this is often the case in relation to home and school selection.

But can parents provide meaningful experience in areas such as physical control of the body, appropriate movement experience, and skill learning? Do they know which activities are best suited to young children, or how to recognize when children are ready to cope with new pursuits?

Sometimes their decision is a reaction to peer pressure or to current vogues, sometimes it is influenced by constraints on quality time together as a family unit. Parents usually make decisions about activity selection on the basis of their participation interests, the local facilities and the complexities of transportation, rather than choosing what would be most beneficial to the children. Questions of who is best placed to provide the chosen experience also tend to dwell on qualification issues rather than on philosophy or principles. This is not the parents' fault, as the majority of information regarding early childhood activity does not often compare the values of contrasting experience, or it is written in literature which is read more by researchers than by parents or coaches. That is why practical information based on research into growth function and early learning is needed.

(Gervis and Brierley 1999, p.9)

Chapter 8

Meet Some 'Graduates' of the Program

John

John was unhappy. He was regularly bullied at school. The other children saw him knock over the furniture in class; they saw him struggle with his writing; they saw him struggle in PE; they saw him as different and thought that this was enough to justify bullying him. John's teachers tried to protect him but they could not be everywhere and the bullies got at John and made him very unhappy. John was bigger than the other boys and physically he could have defended himself, but he lacked self-confidence and when he was bullied he covered his head with his arms and took his punishment.

John was in a class of 30 children who completed the exercise program for six weeks. He worked hard and made excellent progress. At the start of the six weeks he was able to complete one set of ten bench jumps, but when he finished he complained that he was tired and that the muscles on the front of his legs and his lower back were tired, although he recovered fairly quickly.

After just six weeks, John was able to complete four sets of 100 bench jumps with just a 60 second recovery between each set. He no longer complained of feeling tired or of the muscles in his legs and back feeling tired. He enjoyed the exercise and he was pleased with his progress.

The week after the program ended I had to return to the school to meet the principal. I wanted to express my appreciation for her cooperation and feed back to her on the way that the program had gone. On my way to the principal's office I met John. He had a black eye and when I mentioned this to the principal she told me the story. Apparently, John's teachers had noticed a substantial improvement in John's writing and general movement skills. There had also been a consequential improvement in John's self-confidence and when he was targeted for another regular dose of bullying he had decided to defend himself and had seen off the bullies.

Whilst not condoning the use of violence in any way, I must admit to a certain degree of pride in being able to have such a fundamentally positive effect on John's ability to go through life without being bullied.

The program had been designed to eliminate movement difficulties but improving self-confidence is a natural consequence of improved movement skills and can have equally significant benefits for the affected child. I was told that John's improvement in movement skills and self-confidence was reflected in John's schoolwork and in his relationship with his fellow students.

Sophie

Sophie was four and a half years old and she was in the reception class at her local primary school. She had movement difficulties. She could not use scissors to cut paper and when she tried to play with a jigsaw the whole thing landed on the floor. But the problems did not stop there.

When Sophie experienced problems in completing tasks, everybody else knew about it. She would throw things. She would scream. She would hit the nearest person. She would have a tantrum.

Sophie completed the program for six weeks. Being the daughter of middle-aged parents, she had not done much sport or exercise and she enjoyed the chance to stretch her legs and test herself against a class of her peers. She worked hard and the progress was clear for all to see.

It was in the classroom and not the gymnasium or the playing field that the biggest difference was noticed, however. Sophie experienced fewer movement difficulties. Her skills improved and there were fewer accidents and more successes. Life for Sophie's teachers and classmates became calmer and quieter. The outbursts and the tantrums stopped completely.

Not only was Sophie learning more, but so were all the other children in her class, who no longer had to tread carefully in Sophie's presence, fearful of a tantrum or outburst. They also no longer had to deal with all the distractions in class.

References

American Psychiatric Association (2000) *Diagnostic and Statistical Manual of Mental Disorder – Fourth Edition, Text Revision (DSM-IV-TR)*. Washington DC: American Psychiatric Association.

Arnheim, D.D. and Sinclair, W.A. (1979) *The Clumsy Child: A Programme of Motor Therapy*. St. Louis, MI: C.V. Mosby and Company.

Ayres, A.J. (1972) *Sensory Integration and Learning Disorders*. Los Angeles, CA: Western Psychological Services.

BBC (2009) Available at http://news.bbc.co.uk/1/hi/health/ 8425161.stm accessed 27 December 2009.

Baden-Powell, R. (1899) *Aids to Scouting: For N.C.O.s and Men*. London: Gale and Polden.

Baden-Powell, R. (1908) *Scouting for Boys: A Handbook for Instruction in Good Citizenship*. London: Stevens Publishing.

Baechle, T.R. and Earle, R.W. (2008) *Essentials of Strength Training and Conditioning*. Champaign, IL: Human Kinetics Publishers.

Bayley, N. (1969) *Manual for the Bayley Scales of Infant Development*. New York, NY: Psychological Corporation.

Behm, D.G., Faigenbaum, A.D., Falk, B. and Klentrou, P. (2008) 'Canadian Society for Exercise Physiology position paper: resistance training in children and adolescents.' *Applied Physiology, Nutrition and Metabolism, 33,* 3, 547–561.

Bellman, M.H., Lingam, S. and Aukett, A. (1996) *Schedule of Growing Skills II*. Windsor: NFER-Nelson.

Berkey, C.S., Rockett, H.R., Field, A.E., Gillman, M.W. *et al.* (2000) 'Activity, dietary intake, and weight changes in a longitudinal study of preadolescent and adolescent boys and girls.' *Pediatrics 105*, E56.

Biggs, V. (2005) *Caged in Chaos: A Dyspraxic Guide to Breaking Free.* London: Jessica Kingsley Publishers.

Blythe, P. (1992) 'A physical approach to resolving learning difficulties.' Paper presented at the 4th European Conference of Neuro-developmental Delay in Children, Chester.

Boon, M. (2010) *Understanding Dyspraxia: A Guide for Parents and Teachers* (2nd edition). London: Jessica Kingsley Publishers.

Boon, M. (2002) *Helping Children with Dyspraxia.* London: Jessica Kingsley Publishers.

Booth, S.L., Sallis, J.F., Ritenbaugh, C., Hill, J.O. *et al.* (2001) 'Environmental and societal factors affect food choice and physical activity: rationale, influences, and leverage points.' *Nutrition Reviews, 59,* S21–S39.

Bouchard, C., Ping, A., Rice, T., Skinner, J., *et al.* (1999) 'Familial aggregation of VO2 max response to exercise training results from the Heritage Family Study'. *Journal of Applied Physiology 87*, 3, 1003–1008.

Branta, C., Haubenstricker, J. and Seefeldt, V. (1984) 'Age changes in motor skills during childhood and adolescence.' *Exercise Sports Sciences Review, 12,* 1, 467–520. In Washington, R.L., Bernhardt, D.T., Gomez, J., Johnson, M.D., *et al.* (2001) 'Committee on Sports Medicine and Fitness and Committee on School Health, Organized Sports for Children and Preadolescents.' *Pediatrics 107,* 6, 1459–1462.

British Medical Journal (1962) 'Clumsy children.' *British Medical Journal 2*, 1665–1666.

Brookes, G. (2007a) *Dyspraxia* (Special Educational Needs). London: Continuum International Publishing Group Ltd.

Brookes, G. (2007b) *The Teaching Assistant's Guide to Dyspraxia.* London: Continuum International Publishing Group Ltd.

Bruininks, R.H. (1978) *Bruininks-Oseretsky Test of Motor Proficiency: Examiner's Manual.* American Guidance Service. ASIN: B0006CZOY4.

Chandler, T.J., Kibler, W.B., Stracener, E.C., Ziegler, A.K., Pace, B. (1992) 'Shoulder strength, power, and endurance in college tennis players.' *American Journal of Sports Medicine, 20,* 4, 455–458.

Colley, M. (2006) *Living with Dyspraxia: A Guide for Adults with Developmental Dyspraxia.* London: Jessica Kingsley Publishers.

Collins English Dictionary. Glasgow: HarperCollins.

Cooper, R.A., Quatrano, L.A., Axelson, P.W., Harlan, W., *et al.* (1999) 'Research on physical activity and health among people with disabilities: a consensus statement.' *Journal of Rehabilitation Research and Development 36,* 142–154.

Coster, W., Deeney, T., Haltiwanger, J. and Haley, S. (1998) *School Function Assessment.* San Antonio, TX: Psychological Corporation.

Crawford, S., Wilson, B.N., and Dewey, D. (2001) 'Identifying developmental coordination disorder: Consistency between tests'. *Physical and Occupational Therapy in Pediatrics, 20,* 29–50.

Croisier, J.-L., Forthomme, B., Namurois, M.-H., Vanderthommen, M., Crielaard, J.-M. (2002). 'Hamstring muscle strain recurrence and strength performance disorders.' *American Journal of Sports Medicine 30, 2,* 199–203.

Davis, W.E. and Burton, A.W. (1991) 'Ecological task analysis: translating movement behaviour theory into practice'. *Adapted Physical Activity Quarterly, 8,* 154–77.

Department of Education and Science (1980) *Safety Series No. 4.* London: Her Majesty's Stationery Office. In Hamill, B.P. (1994) 'Relative safety of weightlifting and weight training.' *Journal of. Strength and Conditioning Research 8,* 1, 53–57.

Dick, F.W. (2003) *Sports Training Principles.* London: A&C Black Publishers Ltd.

Enoka, R.M. (1994) *Neuromechanical Basis of Kinesiology.* Champaign, IL: Human Kinetics Publishers.

FSA (2009) Available at www.food.gov.uk/foodlabelling accessed 27 December 2009.

Faigenbaum, A.D. and Westcott, W.L. (2000) *Strength and Power for Young Athletes.* Champaign, IL: Human Kinetics Publishers.

Faigenbaum, A.D., Kraemer, W.J., Cahill, B., Chandler, J., *et al.* (1996). 'Youth resistance training: Position statement paper and literature review.' *Strength and Conditioning Journal 18,* 6, 62–75.

Farnham-Diggory, S. (1992) *The Learning Disabled Child.* Cambridge, MA: Harvard University Press.

Folio, M.R. and Fewell R.R. (2000) *Peabody Developmental Motor Scales.* Therapy Skill Builders.

Frankenburg, W.K. and Dodds, J.B. (1967) 'The Denver Developmental Screening Test'. *Journal of Paediatrics, 71,* 181–91.

Frankenburg, W.K., Dodds, J., Archer, P. and Bresnick, B. (1990) *Denver II Technical Manual.* Denver, CO: Denver Developmental Materials Inc.

Gallahue, D.L. and Ozmun, J.C. (1995) *Understanding Motor Development* (3rd edition) Madison, WI: Brown & Benchmark.

Gervis, M. and Brierley, J. (1999) *Effective Coaching for Children: Understanding the Sports Process.* Marlborough: Crowood Press.

Geuze, R. (2007) *Developmental Coordination Disorder: A Review of Current Approaches.* Marseille: Solal Editeurs.

Griffiths, R. (1970) *The Abilities of Young Children: A Comprehensive System of Mental Measurement for the First Eight Years of Life.* London: Child Development Research Centre.

Hadders-Algra, M. (2003) 'Developmental coordination disorder: Is clumsy motor behavior caused by a lesion of the brain at early age?' *Neural Plasticity 10*, 39–50.

Haley, S.M., Coster, W.J., Ludlow, L.H., Haltiwanger, J.T. and Andrellos, P.J. (1992) *Pediatric Evaluation of Disability Inventory (PEDI): Development, Standardisation and Administration Manual.* London: The Psychological Corporation.

Hamill, B.P. (1994) 'Relative safety of weightlifting and weight training.' *Journal of Strength and Conditioning Research, 8,* 1, 53–57.

Haubenstricker, J., Seefeldt, V., Fountain, C. and Sapp, M. (1981) 'The efficiency of the Bruininks-Oseretsky Test of Motor Proficiency in discriminating between normal children and those with gross motor dysfunction'. *Paper presented at the Motor Development Academy at the AAHPERD Convention, Boston, MA.*

Haywood, K.M. and Getchell, N. (2005) *Life Span Motor Development.* Champaign, IL: Human Kinetics Publishers.

Heiser, T.M., Weber, J., Sullivan, G., Clare, P. and Jacobs, R.R. (1984) 'Prophylaxis and management of hamstring muscle injuries in intercollegiate football players.' *American Journal of Sports Medicine 12,* 5, 368–370.

Henderson, S.E. and Sugden. D.A. (1992) *Movement Assessment Battery for Children.* London: The Psychological Corporation.

Kennedy, J.F. (1960) *The Soft American.* Speech by John F. Kennedy on 26 December.

Keogh, J.F. (1982) 'The Study of Movement Learning Disabilities'. In J.P. Das, R.F. Mulcahy and A.E. Wall (eds.), *Theory and Research in Learning Disabilities.* New York, NY: Plenum Press.

Kirby, A. and Drew, S. (2003) *Guide to Dyspraxia and Developmental Coordination Disorders.* London: David Fulton Publishers.

Kolata, G. (2002) 'Why some people won't be fit despite exercise'. New York Times 12 December 2002. Available at http://query.nytimes.com/gst/fullpage.html?res=946EEDE113CF931A25751COA9649C8B63&sec=health. Accessed 24 February 2011.

Kraemer, W.J. and Fleck, S.J. (1993) *Strength Training for Young Athletes*. Champaign, IL: Human Kinetics Publishers.

Kurtz, L.A. (2008) *Understanding Motor Skills in Children with Dyspraxia, ADHD, Autism, and Other Learning Disabilities: A Guide to Improving Coordination*. London: Jessica Kingsley Publishers.

Laszlo, J.I. and Bairstow, P.J. (1985) *Kinaesthetic Sensitivity Test*. Perth, WA: Senkit PTY in association with London: Holt, Rinehart and Winston.

Lee, M.G. and Smith, G.N. (1998) 'The effectiveness of physiotherapy for dyspraxia.' *Physiotherapy, 84,* 276–284.

Lehmkuhle, K. and Williams, M. (1993) 'Defective visual pathway in dyslexics.' *New England Journal of Medicine 328,* 989–995.

Livingstone, M.S., Rosen, G.D., Drislane, F.W., and Galaburda, A.M. (1991) 'Physiological and anatomical evidence for a magnocellular defect in developmental dyslexia.' *Proceedings of the National Academy of Science of the USA 88,* 18, 7943–7947.

Loovis, E.M. and Ersing, W.F. (1979) *Assessing and Programming Gross Motor Development for Children*. Bloomington, Indiana: Tichenor Publishing.

Macintyre, C. (2002) *Dyspraxia in the Early Years: Identifying and Supporting Children with Movement Difficulties*. London: David Fulton Publishers.

Magill, R.A. (2003) *Motor Learning and Control: Concepts and Applications*. New York: McGraw Hill Education.

Martens, R., Christina, R.W., Harvey, J.S. and Sharkey, B.J. (1981) *Coaching Young Athletes*. Champaign, IL: Human Kinetics Publishers.

McClenaghan, B.A. and Gallahue, D.L. (1978) *Observation and Assessment*. Philadelphia, PA: WB. Saunders.

McClenaghan, B.A. (1976) *Development of an Observational Instrument to Assess Selected Fundamental Movement Patterns of Low Motor Functioning Children*. Unpublished Doctoral Dissertation, Indiana University.

McCreight, B. (1997) *Recognizing and Managing Children with Fetal Alcohol Syndrome/Fetal Alcohol Effects: A Guidebook*. Washington, DC: CWLA Press.

Nietzsche, F. (1888) *Twilight of Idols and Anti-Christ*. Reprinted in 2003 by Penguin Classics.

Nordau, M.S. (1892) *Degeneration*. London: Heinemann Publishers.

Oliveira, M.A., Loss, J.F., Petersen, R.D.S., Clark, J.E. and Shim, J.K. (2006) 'Kinetic redundancy on hand digit control in children with DCD.' Available at http://www.asbweb.org/conferences/2006/pdfs/142.pdf accessed 30 January 2011.

Oliver, J. (2009) Available at www.jamieoliver.com/school-dinners accessed 27 December 2009.

Orton, S. J. (1937) *Reading, Writing and Speech Problems in Children.* New York: Norton.

Pearson, D., Falgenbaum, A., Conley, M. and Kraemer, W.J. (2000) 'The National Strength and Conditioning Association's Basic Guidelines for the Resistance Training of Athletes.' *Journal of the National Strength and Conditioning Association 22,* 4, 14–27.

Piaget, J. (1962) 'Play, dreams, and imitation in childhood.' New York: W.W. Norton. In Rowland, T.W. (2007) 'Promoting physical activity for children's health.' *Sports Medicine. 37,* 11, 929–936.

Platt, G.K. (2010) Unpublished doctoral dissertation. Edinburgh: University of Edinburgh.

Pollard, I. (2007) 'Neuropharmacology of drugs and alcohol in mother and fetus.' *Seminars in Fetal and Neonatal Medicine, 12,* 106–113.

Pomeroy, S.B., Burstein, S.M., Donlan, W. and Roberts, J.T. (2009) *A Brief History of Ancient Greece: Politics, Society and Culture.* Oxford: Oxford University Press.

Raynor, A.J. (1989) *The Running Pattern of Seven Year Old Children: Coordination and Gender Differences.* (BPD Honours thesis). Nedlands, Australia: University of Western Australia.

Raynor, A.J. (2001). 'Strength, power, and coactivation in children with developmental coordination disorder.' *Developmental Medicine and Child Neurology 43,* 676–684.

Roach, E.G. and Kephart, N.C (1966) *The Purdue Perceptual Motor Survey (PPMS).* USA: Charles E. Merrill Publishing Co.

Rowland, T.W. (2007) 'Promoting physical activity for children's health.' *Sports Medicine 37,* 11, 929–936.

Rugby Football Union (1990) *6th Report on Injuries.* Twickenham: Rugby Football Union. In Hamill, B.P. (1994) 'Relative safety of weightlifting and weight training.' *Journal of. Strength and Conditioning Research 8,* 1, 53–57.

Sandercock, G., Voss, C., McConnell, D. and Rayner, P. (2010) 'Ten year declines in the cardiorespiratory fitness of affluent English children are largely independent of changes in body mass index.' *Archives of Disease in Childhood 95,* 46–47.

Seefeldt, V. and Haubenstricker, J. (1976) *Developmental Sequences of Fundamental Motor Skills.* Unpublished research, Michigan State University.

Schmidt, R.A. and Wrisberg, C.A., (2008) *Motor Learning and Performance: A Problem-based Learning Approach.* Champaign, IL: Human Kinetics Publishers.

Schraw, G., Crippen, K.J. and Hartley, K. (2006) 'Promoting self-regulation in science education: metacognition as part of a broader perspective of learning.' *Research in Science Education 36,* 111–139.

Simeonsson, R.J., McMillen, J.S. and Huntington, G.S. (2002) 'Secondary conditions in children with disabilities: spina bifida as a case example.' *Mental Retardation and Developmental Disabilities Research Reviews 8,* 198–205.

Smith, A. and Biddle, S.J.H. (2008) *Youth Physical Activity and Sedentary Behaviour: Challenges and Solutions.* Champaign, IL: Human Kinetics Publishers.

State, O. (1955) *Weight Training For Athletics.* London: Amateur Athletic Association.

Steele, C.A., Kalnins, L.V., Jutai, J.W., Stevens, S.E., Bortolussi, J.A. and Biggar, W.D. (1996) 'Lifestyle health behaviors of 11- to 16-year-old youth with physical disabilities.' *Health Education Research, 11,* 173–186.

Stein, J. (2003) 'Visual motor sensitivity and reading.' *Neuropsychologica, 41,* 1785–1793.

Stone, M.H., Stone, M. and Sands, W.A. (2007) *Principles and Practice of Resistance Training.* Champaign, IL: Human Kinetics Publishers.

Stratton, G., Jones, M., Fox, K.R., Tolfrey, K., *et al.* (2004) 'BASES Position Statement on Guidelines for Resistance Exercise in Young People.' *Journal of Sports Sciences 22,* 4, 383–390.

Sugden, D.A. and Wright, H.C. (1998) *Motor Coordination Disorders in Children. Developmental Clinical Psychology and Psychiatry, vol. 30.* London: Sage Publications.

The Independent (2009) Available at http://www.independent.co.uk/news/education/ education-news/ban-on-fast-food-outlets-near-schools-969779.html accessed 27 December 2009.

Touwen, B.C.L. (1979) *Examination of the Child with Minor Neurological Dysfunction. Clinics in Developmental Medicine.* London: SIMP with Heinemann Medical.

Tucker, L. (2002) *An Introductory Guide to Anatomy and Physiology.* Cambridge: Holistic Therapy Books.

Ulrich, D.A. (1985) *Test of Gross Motor Development.* Austin, TX: Pro-Ed. ASIN: B0006EMDCS.

US Department of Health and Human Services (1999) *Promoting Physical Activity.* Champaign, IL: Human Kinetics Publishers.

van der Ploeg, H.P., van der Beek, A.J., van der Woude, L.H.V. and van Mechelen, W. (2004) 'Physical activity for people with a disability: a conceptual model.' *Sports Medicine, 34,* 639–649.

Victor, J.D., Conte, M.M., Burton, L., and Nass, R.D. (1993) 'VEPs in dyslexics and normals: failure to find difference in transient or steady state responses.' *Vision Neuroscience 10*, 939–946.

Walker, B. (2004) 'The FITT Principle in relation to injury prevention.' *Brian Mackenzie's Successful Coaching.* Available at www.brianmac.co.uk/articles/scni15al.htm

Washington, R.L., Bernhardt, D.T., Gomez, J., Johnson, M.D., *et al.* (2001) 'Committee on Sports Medicine and Fitness and Committee on School Health, Organized Sports for Children and Preadolescents.' *Pediatrics 107,* 6, 1459–1462.

WHO (1992) *The ICD-10 Classification of Mental and Behavioural Disorders: Clinical Descriptions and Diagnostic Guidelines.* Geneva: World Health Organization.

Widmaier, E., Raff, H. and Strang, K. (1990) *Human Physiology.* New Castle, DE: McGraw-Hill.

Wislett, U., Ellingsen O. and Kemi O. (2009) 'High-intensity interval training to maximize cardiac benefit of exercise training?'. *Exercise and Sports Sciences Reviews 37*, 3, 139–146.

Zatsiorsky, V.M. and Kraemer, W.J. (2006) *Science and Practice of Strength Training.* Champaign, IL: Human Kinetics.

Subject index

Author Index